THE
DÜNGEONMEISTER
→ BOOK OF ←

RPG
TRIVIA

THE DÜNGEONMEISTER

BOOK OF

RPG TRIVIA

400+ EPIC QUESTIONS TO QUIZ YOUR FRIENDS—AND FOES!

 JEF ALDRICH & JON TAYLOR

Creators of the Düngeonmeister Series

Adams Media

New York   London   Toronto   Sydney   New Delhi

Adams Media
An Imprint of Simon & Schuster, LLC
100 Technology Center Drive
Stoughton, Massachusetts 02072

First Adams Media trade paperback edition September 2024

ADAMS MEDIA and colophon are registered trademarks of Simon & Schuster, LLC.

Simon & Schuster: Celebrating 100 Years of Publishing in 2024

For information about special discounts for bulk purchases, please contact Simon & Schuster Special Sales at 1-866-506-1949 or business@simonandschuster.com.

The Simon & Schuster Speakers Bureau can bring authors to your live event. For more information or to book an event, contact the Simon & Schuster Speakers Bureau at 1-866-248-3049 or visit our website at www.simonspeakers.com.

Interior design by Sylvia McArdle
Illustrations © 123RF

Manufactured in the United States of America

1 2024

Library of Congress Cataloging-in-Publication Data
Names: Aldrich, Jef, author. | Taylor, Jon, 1982- author.
Title: The Düngeonmeister book of RPG trivia / Jef Aldrich & Jon Taylor, creators of the Düngeonmeister series.
Other titles: Düngeonmeister book of role playing game trivia
Description: First Adams Media trade paperback edition. | Stoughton, Massachusetts: Adams Media, [2024] | Series: The Düngeonmeister series
Identifiers: LCCN 2024013260 | ISBN 9781507222805 (pb) | ISBN 9781507222812 (ebook)
Subjects: LCSH: Fantasy games--Miscellanea. | Games--Miscellanea. | Düngeonmeister.
Classification: LCC GV1469.6 .A436 2024 | DDC 793.93--dc23/eng/20240515
LC record available at https://lccn.loc.gov/2024013260

ISBN 978-1-5072-2280-5
ISBN 978-1-5072-2281-2 (ebook)

CONTENTS

INTRODUCTION

Why exactly is it called Vancian casting? Why are there so many games that are Powered by the Apocalypse? What the heck is a Zocchi ball? With *The Düngeonmeister Book of RPG Trivia*, you'll not only learn the answers to these questions; you'll also be able to test your and your gaming group's knowledge on the gigantic world of RPGs and more.

Throughout the book, you'll find ten chapters that cover everything from the history of RPGs to RPGs in media to the humor in many of these games. You'll also be tested on the particulars of famous fantasy worlds, miniature-focused RPGs, role-playing video games, and more! In each chapter, you'll find the following four types of questions that test your RPG knowledge in different ways:

- **Multiple Choice questions** (1 point), where you select the one true answer.
- **True or False questions** (1 point), where you cast the Zone of Truth to determine if the statement sounds either correct or dubious.
- **Open Answer questions** (2 points), where you conjure your answer to fill in the blank that the question provides.
- **Connect the Answer questions** (1 point for 1—3 correct answers, 2 points for 4—6 correct answers, and 3 points for 7 or 8 correct answers), where you create matched pairs from separate lists that ring true (for example, a bard and their mandolin).

Each question will have an answer printed upside down at the bottom of the page. If the satisfaction of a correct answer is enough for you, that's great! Don't worry about keeping score. But if you want to see how well you've done, refer to the point values in the bulleted list. To quiz yourself, you can either check your answers as you go or write your answers down and see how you did at the end. To quiz your friends, designate a Game Master to ask the questions while everyone else records their answers on a blank piece of paper. Score each other's papers at the end of each round using the point values included in the bulleted list.

After you've scored, compare your points to the maximum that you could have received for the chapter. There are some difficult and obscure questions in here, so getting 50 percent or higher is impressive. If you can get 90 percent or more, then you're a super-fan! Additionally, sprinkled throughout the pages of this book, you'll find extra bits of related trivia that we've added to make the subject even more interesting.

So roll an Intelligence check, dive into one of the many interesting categories in this book, get a pen and paper to keep score, and put your mind to the ultimate test of RPG knowledge.

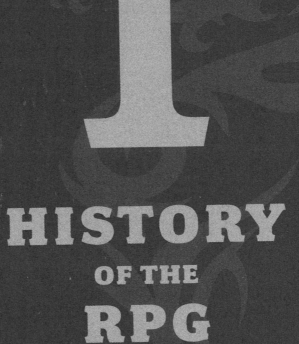

1

HISTORY
OF THE
RPG

Questions about the History and Notable Places, People, and Creatures of Tabletop Role-Play Gaming

Humans have been playing pretend for as long as they've had the ability to communicate. Thankfully, this chapter isn't going to demand you know things about Throg the Caveman and what the first animal he pretended to be was (it was a woolly rhinoceros, obviously). Instead, this chapter will be all about the history of the modern and codified version of playing pretend that we all know and love: role-playing games (RPGs).

RPGs have had a storied past with many big names that influenced the hobby for decades, as well as some lesser-known ones that were just as crucial. Obviously, these games didn't come fully formed from the head of some mythic genius; they have always been influenced by various games, books, and other media. Much of what is associated with RPGs can be traced back to something that that author loved.

In addition to the creators and circumstances that helped to forge our favorite games, this chapter will look at some of the other early role-playing games. Here you'll find questions about games from the seventies and eighties that are still relevant and played today. Regardless of the quality of staying power of these titles, each one is an example of the weird and interesting history of the RPG.

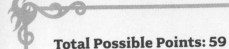

1

Often considered to be the progenitor of what we now consider modern role-playing games, Dungeons & Dragons has had a huge impact on the hobby. In what year was the original *Dungeons & Dragons* game released?

A. 1970   **B.** 1974   **C.** 1978   **D.** 1982

2

In addition to Gary Gygax, who else is credited for the design of Dungeons & Dragons?

Critical Info

The company that published D&D, TSR, was formed by the cocreators of D&D and Don Kaye. Kaye and Gygax would put together the initial copies of D&D in Gygax's basement. Sadly, Kaye suffered a fatal heart attack in 1975 and never got to see what an impact the game had on the world.

1. B. 1974. 2. Dave Arneson.

3

It took less than a year after *D&D* came out for someone to try to make it more accessible, and this game would become *D&D*'s earliest competitor. What was that game?

A. *Basements and Balrogs*

B. *Caves and Carnosaurs*

C. *Bridges and Beasts*

D. *Tunnels & Trolls*

4

True or false?: Vancian casting is named after the character Vance from the Dying Earth books.

5

Inspired by *Watership Down*, what early RPG positions the players in the role of rabbits trying to survive predation, starvation, and every other horror that might befall a harmless rodent?

3. D. *Tunnels & Trolls.* 4. False. It's named after the author of Dying Earth, Jack Vance. 5. *Bunnies and Burrows.*

11

6

Wargaming rules were initially used as the basis for the Dungeons & Dragons rules and were heavily ingrained in the initial books. Assume you already had a copy of the wargame rules to reference. What was that wargame called?

A. *Chainmail*

B. *Medieval Marches*

C. *Polearm*

D. *Castle Crashers*

7

True or false?: The first superhero RPG to be released was *Heroes Unlimited* by Palladium Games.

8

One of the first RPGs, which came out the same year as *Dungeons & Dragons*, was set in M.A.R. Barker's Tékumel universe. Barker had written thousands of pages of history for this universe and even created its own language. What was the RPG called?

A. *Tékumel: The World Beyond*

B. *The Golden Age*

C. *Empire of the Petal Throne*

D. *The Land of Sun and Wind*

6. A. Chainmail. 7. False. It was Superhero: 2044. 8. C. Empire of the Petal Throne.

12

9

The *Deities and Demigods* book for *Advanced Dungeons & Dragons* was full of gods and monsters that you could include in your game. Unfortunately, it also included some gods and monsters that were copyrighted and included without permission. What needed to be hastily removed from later printings of this book?

A. Cthulhu
B. Gandalf
C. The Wizard of Oz
D. A very Marvel-looking version of Thor

10

True or false?: The alignment system of D&D is inspired by the cosmology of the Elric stories by Michael Moorcock.

Critical Info

While the 9-point alignment grid is the most famous of the versions, D&D has had several versions. The original had 3 alignments (lawful, chaotic, and neutral); the 4th edition had 5 (good, lawful good, evil, chaotic evil, and unaligned), and the 5th edition has 10 (the standard 9-point axis as well as the unaligned option).

9. A. Cthulh. 10. True.

11

RPGs have been using licensed settings for a long time in order to allow players to explore their favorite worlds from popular media. What was the first RPG license that was based on a television show?

A. *Star Trek*

B. *Doctor Who*

C. *Buffy the Vampire Slayer*

D. *Lost in Space*

12

While traveling through the settings of popular books and TV shows is great, gamers also love to embody characters in beloved blockbuster movies. What was the first RPG license that was based on a movie?

A. *Indiana Jones*

B. *Ghostbusters*

C. *Star Wars*

D. *James Bond*

13

In *Advanced Dungeons & Dragons 2nd Edition*, the armor class (AC) of a foe was such that a lower AC was better and went from 10 to −10. The acronym for the calculation of what you needed to roll was known as what?

14

Dungeons & Dragons has had plenty of settings over the years, spanning all kinds of genres from standard fantasy to sci-fi to horror. What was the first published setting for D&D?

A. *Blackmoor*

B. *Forgotten Realms*

C. *Greyhawk*

D. *Dragonlance*

15

True or false?: The company TSR that first published D&D is an acronym that stands for Tactical Studies Rules.

16

While TSR dominated the early RPG publishing sector thanks to D&D, plenty of other companies sprung up in the early seventies and eighties, and many are still around to this day. One of the biggest and earliest ones was *Chaosium*. What was the first RPG that the fledgling company ever published?

A. *Call of Cthulhu*

B. *RuneQuest*

C. *Stormbringer*

D. *7th Sea*

17

True or false?: The original *Dungeons & Dragons* didn't have non-combat skills and wouldn't until they were introduced in *AD&D 2nd Edition Dungeon Master's Guide.*

18

D&D borrowed heavily from various sources, such as J.R.R. Tolkien, but the widespread use of which term from the Lewis Carroll poem "Jabberwocky" would define the early editions' most powerful sword?

19

Many designers have long desired the ability to make a system that could fit any player or Game Master's needs. This goal gave rise to the first generic RPG systems that were setting agnostic and allowed the players to build whatever they wanted. What was the first of these universal systems?

A. *GURPS*

B. *Basic Role Playing*

C. *Hero System*

D. *TWERPS*

17. False. Skills were first introduced in 1985's *Oriental Adventures.* 18. Vorpal. 19. B. *Basic Role Playing.*

16

Dungeons & Dragons is known for having a highly developed and broad cosmology with pantheons that include gods specifically for most species in the game. Match the D&D species with one of their gods.

A. Goblins

B. Gnolls

C. Drow

D. Halflings

E. Beholders

F. Dwarves

G. Orcs

H. Kuo-toa

1. Moradin

2. Lolth

3. Gruumsh

4. Yeenoghu

5. Gzemnid

6. Maglubiyet

7. Blibdoolpoolp

8. Yondalla

A small but vocal group of concerned parents and public figures began to blame D&D and other RPGs for many real-world problems; they believed the games would teach children witchcraft and demon summoning. What was this time period called?

Critical Info

The anti-RPG advocacy group BADD (Bothered About Dungeons & Dragons) described the game as "a fantasy role-playing game which uses demonology, witchcraft, voodoo, murder, rape, blasphemy, suicide, assassination, insanity, sex perversion, homosexuality, prostitution, satanic type rituals, gambling, barbarism, cannibalism, sadism, desecration, demon summoning, necromantics, divination and other teachings."

One of the early entries from Chaosium that still exists today is a game based on Arthurian legend. The game envisions the players as knights and can even span generations of a family with titles and lands passed down. What is the name of this game?

A. *The Arthurian Legends*

B. *Heroes of the Round Table*

C. *Pendragon*

D. *Knights and Knaves*

There have been plenty of prolific, talented writers and game designers from the seventies and eighties that created the influential systems and settings used to this day. Match the game designer with one of their most influential games. (Note that many of these people have worked on more than one of these games. This game is the one for which they were the primary, original creator.)

A. Greg Stafford

B. Steve Jackson

C. Steve Perrin

D. Gary Gygax

E. Sandy Petersen

F. Kevin Siembieda

G. James M. Ward

H. Ken St. Andre

1. *Gamma World*

2. *Dungeons & Dragons*

3. *Pendragon*

4. *Tunnels & Trolls*

5. *RuneQuest*

6. *GURPS*

7. *Call of Cthulhu*

8. *Heroes Unlimited*

23. A. Greg Stafford & 3. Pendragon. B. Steve Jackson & 6. GURPS. C. Steve Perrin & 5. RuneQuest. D. Gary Gyxax & 2. Dungeons & Dragons. E. Sandy Petersen & 7. Call of Cthulhu. F. Kevin Siembieda & 8. Heroes Unlimited. G. James M. Ward & 1. Gamma World. H. Ken St. Andre & 4. Tunnels & Trolls.

24

TSR, fearful of unwanted media attention and not wanting to upset any worried mothers, couldn't include Demons and Devils in the *Advanced Dungeons & Dragons 2nd Edition Monstrous Manual*. So rather than drop them entirely, they just renamed both groups of monsters. What were those creatures changed to?

A. Fiends and Hellions

B. Imps and Gremlins

C. Daemons and Dyvils

D. Tanar'ri and Baatezu

25

True or false?: *AD&D* had plenty of random tables and charts for the DM to use, including a chart that you could roll on monthly to see if your players randomly contracted a parasitic infection.

26

What game is set in a comical, dystopian future city where everything is under the watchful eye of "Friend Computer" and is heavily influenced by works like *1984* and *Brave New World* but with a dark humor to it?

27

Though Gary Gygax spent his life on an FBI watchlist, it wasn't his RPG publishing company that was raided by the secret service. What company made the government nervous enough to send in personnel?

A. Steve Jackson Games

B. Amarillo Design Bureau

C. Palladium Games

D. Presidential Assassination Games

Critical Info

The reason for the raid had to do with an upcoming *Cyberpunk* book the company was putting out. Turns out doing research on hacking and computer security, even if completely lawful, means your book might be teaching people how to do real computer crimes. That's why we (the authors) avoided doing any coding research for this book. Better safe than sorry!

28

True or false?: RPGs became so influential when they came out that they started sneaking their way into all sorts of other mediums. This includes the creation of the choose-your-own-adventure—type books that were made as solitaire RPGs.

27. A. Steve Jackson Games. 28. True.

29

Most early games would follow in D&D's footsteps for character creation, where you use dice to randomize your statistics and then flesh your character out around that random creation. While many games would include optional point-buy systems for certain things like attributes, what was the first game to make point-buy the default choice for every aspect of character creation?

A. GURPS

B. Fantasy Hero

C. Champions

D. Justice, Inc.

30

While the first RPGs were primarily made and marketed in the US, it didn't take long for other countries to both import these games and begin making some of their own. What game was made in 1984 and is the most successful role-playing game in the German market, outselling even *Dungeons & Dragons*?

A. Mysterious Lands

B. The Dark Eye

C. Forest Rangers

D. The Name of God

29. C. Champions. 30. B. The Dark Eye.

31

True or false?: The first box set for *Dungeons & Dragons* came in a magenta box depicting a green dragon fighting two adventurers.

32

True or false?: TSR published their first city setting, City State of the Invincible Overlord, which was a dwarven fortress meant to be used as either a base of operations or the start of a city-based adventure.

33

True or false?: *Traveller* is one of the earliest sci-fi RPGs where players could use a robust character creation system that wouldn't just tell them their statistics; it would also reveal the history of the character and how they got those skills. It was so robust in storytelling that players could die during character creation.

31. False. It was a blue box with a red dragon. 32. False. While compatible with D&D, the setting was published by Judges Guild. 33. True.

23

34

One of the earliest RPG settings that predates even the RPG itself is Glorantha. It has a lot of fascinating races, but it is definitely most famous for the duck people that look like they are straight out of a Saturday morning cartoon. What are they called?

A. The Durulz

B. The Quack Pack

C. The Anatidae

D. The Rhyncos

35

TSR attempted to release another role-playing game in the early days with a very different genre. Trying to capitalize on America's love of cowboys, they put out a western-themed RPG with an entirely different system than D&D. What was the name of that game?

36

With a focus on combat, inclusion of teams with highly trained individuals, and a background stemming from historical reenactment, it's only natural that RPGs would eventually move to focus on modern warfare. *Behind Enemy Lines* was the first RPG to be set during what real world war?

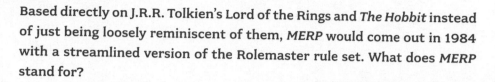

37

Based directly on J.R.R. Tolkien's Lord of the Rings and *The Hobbit* instead of just being loosely reminiscent of them, *MERP* would come out in 1984 with a streamlined version of the Rolemaster rule set. What does *MERP* stand for?

38

True or false?: *Gangster!* is a role-playing game set in Chicago during the Prohibition Era of the 1920s where players could choose to be either on the side of the law or criminals.

39

Ars Magica was the first game to coin the phrase "troupe system" as it pertains to how to run a game. What does running a game with a troupe system mean?

37. *Middle-earth Role Playing.* 38. True. 39. Each player takes on different roles of NPCs at different times, rather than the GM acting as all NPCs.

25

The history of RPGs is littered with all sorts of firsts. Can you match up the game with the historic first that it represents?

A. First cross-genre RPG

B. First Japanese-language RPG

C. First comedy RPG

D. First published LARP

E. First German-language RPG

F. First generic (no-setting) RPG

G. First sci-fi RPG

H. First anime RPG

1. *Donkey Commando*

2. *Killer*

3. *Metamorphosis Alpha*

4. *Arduin*

5. *Alma Mater*

6. *BRP*

7. *Mekton*

8. *Midgard*

40. A. First cross-genre RPG & 4. *Arduin*. B. First Japanese-language RPG & 1. *Donkey Commando*. C. First comedy RPG & 5. *Alma Mater*. D. First published LARP & 2. *Killer*. E. First German-language RPG & 8. *Midgard*. F. First generic (no-setting) RPG & 6. *BRP*. G. First sci-fi RPG & 3. *Metamorphosis Alpha*. H. First anime RPG & 7. *Mekton*.

Critical Info

Dungeons & Dragons is often cited as being the first role-playing game, but the point at which a game stops being something else and starts being an RPG is sort of nebulous. The inspiration for *D&D* was Braunstein wargaming, where people were playing a role in their game. However, the line that separates "wargame with role-playing aspects" from "role-playing game with wargame aspects" is blurry at best.

41

True or false?: Palladium Games published *Rifts* in 1990, increasing the power level of the world and its threats so much that a third form of damage, scaled much larger than the existing hit points and SDC, was added. This game had hit points, structural damage capacity (SDC), and introduced mega damage capacity (MDC), which was worth 100 SDC per point.

42

In 1984, Chaosium released a game based on the comic by Wendy and Richard Pini set on the World of the Two Moons. In this game, players could take on the roles of the elves from the main series like Cutter, Skywise, and Redlance. What is the name of the comic/RPG?

41. True. 42. Elfquest

2

TOOLS
OF THE
TRADE

Questions about Dice, Character Sheets, and the DM's Pizza

Should you ever brave a gaming convention, you'll undoubtedly find all manner of crowds, lines, as well as crushes and throngs of bodies, though few will ever match the consistent intensity of the fracas of people in front of a dice store. These ever-popular randomizing tools have been a ubiquitous feature of the RPG industry for as long as there has been one, and of the gaming industry for nearly as long as gambling has existed. In fact, museums today hold dice discovered from antiquity that exceed two thousand years of age!

Modern dice are available in a dizzying array of shapes, sizes, colors, makes, and more. Would you like clear acrylic dice filled with tiny rubber ducks? Easy! A heavy D6 carved from the femur of a woolly mammoth? Perhaps not in the best taste archaeologically speaking, but probably available at one point or another. Modern gamers are presented with a near endless array of options for how to personalize their game space and express themselves artistically and practically. Express yourself with dice, dice towers, spinners, special dice bags, DM screens, or entire bespoke gaming tables with sliding cupholders and hidden TV screens built into the table for displaying maps. You name it, and chances are it has already been monetized by some enterprising manufacturer.

This chapter gets into the weeds of all the different gaming tools you're likely to encounter in RPGs (and some you probably won't ever see).

Total Possible Points: 58

1

Each of the dice (or other randomizing tools) listed below is the sole random tool used by one of the accompanying games. Can you connect them correctly?

A. D10

B. D6

C. Dominoes

D. Playing cards

E. Percentile dice

F. Fudge dice

G. Fortune, Source, Vision, and Quest cards

H. Rock Paper Scissors

1. *Shadowrun*

2. *Aces & Eights*

3. *Noumenon*

4. *FATE*

5. *Werewolf: The Apocalypse*

6. *Mind's Eye Theatre*

7. *Marvel Super Heroes*

8. *Everway*

1. A. D10 & 5. *Werewolf: The Apocalypse* B. D6 & 1. *Shadowrun* C. Dominoes & 3. *Noumenon* D. Playing cards & 2. *Aces & Eights*. E. Percentile dice & 7. *Marvel Super Heroes*. F. Fudge dice & 4. FATE. G. Fortune, Source, Vision, and Quest cards & 8. *Everway*. H. Rock Paper Scissors & 6. *Mind's Eye Theatre*.

2

Sets of dice, including shapes besides the humble six-sided die, are often referred to by what name?

A. Sheep Bones

C. Polyhedral

B. The Numeraries

D. A Myriad

3

How many possible results are there from rolling a "D66" as found in several games, generated by rolling a pair of D6 dice and treating one as the tens digit and the other as the ones digit of a randomly generated result (i.e., a roll of a 3 and 5 would produce the number 35).

4

What is the only die regularly used in the World of Darkness series initially published by White Wolf, including *Vampire: The Masquerade*, *Mage: The Ascension*, and *Hunter: The Vigil*?

5

History's first-known 20-sided die certainly sounds like a magical object in its own right. It is well over two thousand years old, carved from serpentine stone in Ptolemaic Egypt around 300–30 B.C.E., and was likely used for a long-forgotten game of chance or perhaps ancient divination rituals. The die is also not carved with numbers on its faces. What is carved on each face instead?

A. Hieroglyphs
B. Images of Egyptian gods and goddesses
C. Greek letters
D. Advertisements for ancient Egyptian street restaurants

6

True or false?: There are no five, seven, or three-sided dice.

7

True or false?: Secret doors are generally indicated in old dungeon map keys by drawing an S over the line that indicated a door or portal between two dungeon rooms.

5. C. Greek letters. 6. False. These dice, while less commonly used and definitely not platonic solids, are available in a variety of styles. 7. True.

The invention of this tool, invaluable to math nerds since its 1794 patent and to devious dungeon designers since the 1970s, is generally attributed to a Dr. Buxton of England, a name rendered a mononym by the obscuring mists of history.

A. Graph paper
B. The pencil eraser
C. Metric/imperial printed ruler
D. Liquid paper corrective fluid

9

The mechanical pencil would be introduced to the world in 1822 and would over the next 150 years become the standard tool for careful drawing of maps and creepy skeletons. The patent for this invention of a hollow shaft with a lead storage space and screw mechanism for advancing the lead belongs to which two English gentlemen?

A. Screamin' Jay Hawkins and Mordin Solus
B. Sampson Mordan and John Isaac Hawkins
C. Uriah Heep and George Canning
D. Lord Wembley Greystoke Penistone and Sir Downton Abbey, Esq.

8. A. Graph paper. 9. B. Sampson Mordan and John Isaac Hawkins.

10

What 1986 role-playing game made by West End Games introduced "the Ghost die," a special D6 that had alternate results if it came up 1 or 6 during gameplay to facilitate the introduction of chaotic or haunted new elements of the action?

11

True or false?: The D10 was invented by Harold Allan Clarke, lead singer of the 1970s rock group The Hollies.

12

Designed and marketed by historical wargame designer and RPG author Lou Zocchi, the Zocchi ball is actually the largest of several nonstandard RPG dice of his invention. How many faces does a Zocchi ball have?

A. 30

B. 60

C. 100

D. 1, it is an actual ball

10. *Ghostbusters RPG.* 11. False. There are a few people that claim to have invented the modern D10, but all that is known for certain is that it was marketed first by dice company Gamescience in 1980. 12. C. 100.

13

Used in some RPG circles, the Rider-Waite Tarot deck is now considered a tool of the trade. How many cards are in a standard Rider-Waite Tarot deck's major arcana?

14

True or false?: West End Games' classic the *Star Wars RPG* uses a pool-based system that involves rolling only D6 dice, often in significant handfuls.

15

In *AD&D*, player characters would most often interact with the game's maps via a square grid for things like tracking movement, facing, and the size of bursts and blasts from spell effects. They would also switch to a hex-style grid of six-sided adjacent sections when handling overland travel or general land exploration, or in what other combat scenario?

13. 78. 14. True. 15. Aerial combat.

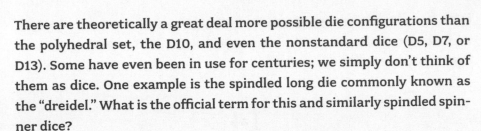

16

There are theoretically a great deal more possible die configurations than the polyhedral set, the D10, and even the nonstandard dice (D5, D7, or D13). Some have even been in use for centuries; we simply don't think of them as dice. One example is the spindled long die commonly known as the "dreidel." What is the official term for this and similarly spindled spinner dice?

A. Top Randomizers

B. Beyblayesian Solids

C. Teetotum

D. Gambletwirlers

Critical Info

The first board game to be manufactured by Milton Bradley, released in 1860 under the name The Checkered Game of Life (which still exists today in a modified form known as Life), was similar to many existing parlor games of the day, insofar as being designed with an eye toward strong moral lessons. In fact, in an attempt to distance the game from the dread vice of gambling, the first printings of The Checkered Game of Life opted instead for a six-sided spindle spinner. Whether the manufacturers realized that these could still be used to play a fairly spinny version of craps is sadly lost to history.

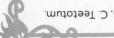

16. C. Teetotum.

17

True or false?: The common name for the standing board printed with art and important game facts that separates the GM's portion of a table from the players' is the DM's Privy.

18

Tarot decks are a fun and fascinating way to engage in the ancient art of cartomancy, which is divining the future from a reading of several drawn cards in a deck. Tarot is still commonly used for divination and fun the world over, but it was originally also used for a wide variety of games, of which only one game still exists in regular play today that makes use of the entire 78-card deck. Which game is it, and in which country is it primarily still played?

A. Husarin and Austria
B. Cups and Coins and England
C. Neunzehnerrufen and Poland
D. Tarok and Denmark

17. False. It's more commonly known as the DM screen, though if a DM is using it as a privy, we don't endorse that or want to know about it. 18. D. Tarok and Denmark.

37

19

There are a wide variety of ways to accomplish the basic task of determining a starting statistic from 3–18 for a game of *Dungeons & Dragons*. Can you connect each of the listed method names to its description on the opposite page?

A. *AD&D 2nd Edition*, Method I

B. *AD&D 2nd Edition*, Method II

C. *AD&D 2nd Edition*, Method III

D. *AD&D 2nd Edition*, Method IV

E. *AD&D 2nd Edition*, Method V

F. *AD&D 2nd Edition*, Method VI

G. *D&D 5th Edition*, Standard

H. Array Unearthed Arcana Method

19. A. *AD&D 2nd Edition*, Method I & 3. 3D6 in character sheet order. B. *AD&D 2nd Edition*, Method II & 5. 3D6 in order, roll twice for each ability and keep best result. C. *AD&D 2nd Edition*, Method III & 2. 3D6, arrange as desired. D. *AD&D 2nd Edition*, Method IV & 6. 3D6 rolled twelve times, choose and arrange best six results as desired. E. *AD&D 2nd Edition*, Method V & 8. 4D6, drop lowest die, arrange as desired.

1. **All scores start at 8, roll 7D6, add each single die result to whatever ability you like; multiple dice can go to one ability; no stat may exceed 18.**

2. **3D6, arrange as desired**

3. **3D6 in character sheet order**

4. **In stat order as determined by character class, roll 9 dice, then 8, then 7, etc. down to 3 for last result, keeping best three of each roll.**

5. **3D6 in order, roll twice for each ability and keep best result.**

6. **3D6 rolled twelve times, choose and arrange best six results as desired.**

7. **Arrange 15, 14, 13, 12, 10, and 8 as desired.**

8. **4D6, drop lowest die, arrange as desired.**

F. AD&D 2nd Edition, Method VI & 1. All scores start at 8, roll 7D6, add each single die result to whatever ability you like; multiple dice can go to one ability; no stat may exceed 18. C. D&D 5th Edition, Standard & 7. Arrange 15, 14, 13, 12, 10, and 8 as desired. H. Array Unearthed Arcana Method & 4. In stat order as determined by character class, roll 9 dice, then 8, then 7, etc. down to 3 for last result, keeping best three of each roll.

20

True or false?: Marvel Comics has both licensed their brand to game publishers and published their own RPGs. In 2003, they published a Marvel RPG that used no dice or randomizers of any kind.

Critical Info

Marvel has had so many officially licensed or self-produced RPGs over the years that a great deal of different randomizing schemes have been tried at one time or another, including percentile dice; 3D6, where one die has "Marvel" printed on the number 1 face; and at one point, a custom deck of 100 playing cards in numbers ranging from 1–10 in five suits representing five of the biggest personalities in Marvel, which were used for randomization as well as a sort of prognostication known officially in-game as "aura reading."

21

The Meenlock, a relatively obscure and forgotten monster from the *AD&D Fiend Folio*, was a small bipedal furry horror with a gross insectile mouth and the ability to generate fear in adventurers that come across them, and it routinely appeared in groups of 3—5. What die roll was supposed to be used to generate this result?

20. True. 21. 1D3+2 or 2D2+1.

22

Gamescience, the company founded by Lou Zocchi (of Zocchi ball fame) was integral to both the RPG and wargaming industries in early modern gaming history. Besides such notable historical games as *The Battle of Britain* and *Superhero: 2044*, they also released a great deal of new dice and helped make the modern polyhedral set the ubiquitously standard array of dice known today. Which die did they first release in 1980? Hint: It's a truncated trapezohedron!

A. D6

B. D10

C. D12

D. The Zocchi ball

23

True or false?: It was once common practice in England to switch the in-game value of Kings and Queens in ordinary decks of playing cards to reflect which manner of monarch currently occupied the crown.

24

LARP, or live-action role playing, is a sort of RPG played not at a table but up and walking around, with players seeking to fully inhabit their character and act as them at all times. Because of this, dice and other randomizing tools can be seen as breaking the immersion, and are often replaced when a random result for a victory between two players is needed. What common schoolyard game is most often substituted?

25

True or false?: *Savage Worlds*, a game produced by Pinnacle Entertainment Group, uses both dice and cards, though the cards are only utilized for dramatic results on noncombat skill challenges.

26

What year did New York legislators mandate the cessation of manufacturing children's toys and figures of lead, prompting manufacturers of miniatures across the world to switch to pewter, various white metal alloys, and plastic?

24. Rock, Paper, Scissors. 25. False. The cards have many uses, most prominently as initiative (turn order) indicators. 26. 1993.

27

Early box set editions of *Dungeons & Dragons* (1977 and 1981 releases) came packaged in a box containing a player's book and a Dungeon Master's book, a set of six polyhedral dice, and, mysteriously, a single crayon. What color was the included crayon in the box?

A. Red

B. Black

C. Brown

D. White

28

While we don't know exactly when it began, Senet is the first known board game, played for at least two thousand years throughout the history of ancient Egypt; depicted in frescoes, wall art, and graffiti; and still known from several existing game boards. While we know all the pieces, we still aren't sure how the game was played. Which of the following is not an ancient Egyptian board game?

A. Khaemweset

B. Hounds and Jackals

C. Backgammon

D. Mehen

27. D. White. 28. C. Backgammon.

In 2003, the company Wizards of the Coast (WOTC) released a music album via the Entity Productions label known as *Dungeons & Dragons: Official Roleplaying Soundtrack*, which was meant to be used as background music to accompany play sessions of the game. This album was written and performed entirely by a single band, and WOTC representatives pitched the concept at a game convention. What was the name of that band?

A. Midnight Syndicate

B. Dragon Force

C. The Jolly Bards

D. Prelude to A Sigh

Critical Info

While the *Dungeons & Dragons: Official Roleplaying Soundtrack* was claimed to be the first official soundtrack for *D&D*, this was in fact untrue, as prior to the purchase of TSR by WOTC, a different album had been licensed and published under the name *First Quest: The Music*, which was released by Filmtrax. It was an album released on either cassette or record and came as musical accompaniment to an included module. This was released in 1985, several years before the *Official Roleplaying Soundtrack*, and copies of it are hard to locate today.

30

What is the common term for the roll of a pair of D10s treating one as the tens digit and the other as the ones digit to determine a random number between 1 and 100?

31

True or false?: Games Workshop games such as *Warhammer* and *Warhammer 40,000* make use of a special die that is rolled to indicate where blasts and magical effects deviate to when they are not perfectly accurate on the battlefield. It is known as the scatter die.

32

What miniatures manufacturing company began in a basement in 1988 and was named after the wizard character of a friend of one of the founding members?

33

The 1988 TSR game *Bullwinkle and Rocky Role Playing Party Game* contains a wide variety of fun tools for gameplay in the box, including character standees, character hand puppets, and wacky gameplay cards referencing all manner of elements of the Frostbite Falls milieu of the cartoon. In order to keep the game simple and easy for kids, it eschewed the use of dice, opting instead for which potentially simpler randomizing tool?

A. Coins with Rocky's head on one side and Boris Badenov's head on the other.

B. Dominos featuring the Wossamotta U school emblem.

C. Board-game-style spinners with the heads of various characters printed on them.

D. A windup Dudley Do-Right and Horse that would dart forward and spin randomly until it hit a standing target with a number on it.

33. C. Board-game-style spinners with the heads of various characters printed on them.

46

34

Wizards of the Coast, the company that produced *Dungeons & Dragons* as well as *Magic: The Gathering*, owns a trademark on the symbol that indicates a card should be turned sideways as a marker that it has been used to generate some effect, forcing other card games to come up with their own names for the game mechanic commonly known as what?

Critical Info

Synonyms for turning a card sideways to indicate it has been used or activated are numerous and include kneeling (A Game of Thrones Collectible Card Game), activating (Runebound), exhausting (Descent: Journeys in the Dark), turning (Shadowrun: The Trading Card Game), booting (Deadlands: Doomtown), spending (Warlord: Saga of the Storm), exerting (The Lord of the Rings Trading Card Game), bowing (Legend of the Five Rings: The Card Game), appealing (Mykerinos), tacking (7th Sea Collectible Card Game), tasking (Flagship: Prometheus Unchained), cranking (On the Edge), charging (City of Heroes Collectible Card Game), fatiguing (Hunting Party), committing (Universal Fighting System), rolling (Gundam War), and locking (Warhammer 40,000 Collectible Card Game).

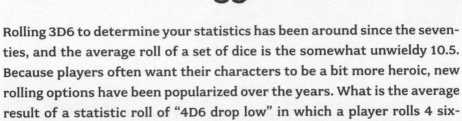

Rolling 3D6 to determine your statistics has been around since the seventies, and the average roll of a set of dice is the somewhat unwieldy 10.5. Because players often want their characters to be a bit more heroic, new rolling options have been popularized over the years. What is the average result of a statistic roll of "4D6 drop low" in which a player rolls 4 six-sided dice and only calculates the combined highest three results?

A. 13.5

B. 11

C. 12.24

D. 14.111

Critical Info

Some dice have been created with more faces, including a few 144-sided, 200-sided, and even numbers painstakingly written into the divots of golf balls to create a 360-sided dice. However, once a die is above a certain value, the utility of both that random number (there's rarely a need to generate a random number between 1 and 360) and the die itself (try rolling a D100 on a slightly slanted table if you want to lose a D100) is not worthwhile.

36

True or false?: The tarot deck at one point had an additional major arcana card known as the Serpent Bearer.

37

What was the intended purpose of the crayon included in early *D&D* box sets from 1977 and 1981?

- **A.** Circling important locations on DM-drawn maps.
- **B.** To color over mistakes in the relatively low-quality book printings.
- **C.** To fill in the etched numbers on the single-color plastic dice.
- **D.** A handy snack for the purchaser's little brother.

38

True or false?: Dice used for craps games in Las Vegas or other cities with legal gambling are manufactured using clear materials to display that they are not loaded or weighed to roll in any particular way.

36. False. If the Serpent Bearer sounds familiar, it's not because it was a lost or forgotten element of tarot, but rather a lost or forgotten constellation of the zodiac and is also known as Ophiuchus. 37. C. To fill in the etched numbers on the single-color plastic dice. 38. True.

39

All these polyhedral dice shapes surely must have science-tastic names attached to them, right? Of course, if you're a gamer you're probably already used to saying "Hey, hand me that D8-shaped thing," but they certainly have names pulled straight from the pages of Euclidian geometry, don't they? Well yes, of course they do. And here's your chance to prove you know how, including some extra fiendish ones!

A. D4

B. D6

C. D8

D. D10

E. D12

F. D20

G. D24

H. D30

1. Pentagonal trapezohedron

2. Dodecahedron

3. Cube

4. Deltoidal icositetrahedron

5. Triangular pyramid

6. Rhombic triacontahedron

7. Icosahedron

8. Octahedron

39. A. D4 & 5. Triangular pyramid. B. D6 & 3. Cube. C. D8 & 8. Octahedron. D. D10 & 1. Pentagonal trapezohedron. E. D12 & 2. Dodecahedron. F. D20 & 7. Icosahedron. G. D24 & 4. Deltoidal icositetrahedron. H. D30 & 6. Rhombic triacontahedron.

50

40

The fair die with the most faces currently manufactured in the world is made by gaming company The Dice Lab, and it can be somewhat tricky to both roll and read without a little practice. It wobbles when rolled, takes some time to settle, and needs to be rotated in place to determine what number is on top. It is also a disdyakis triacontahedron in shape! What number of faces does it have?

A. 100

B. 120

C. 360

D. 1,000

3

FANTASY WORLDS

Questions about Classic Fantasy RPG Adventures

A large part of the gaming experience is in the players' hands. The characters that they make and the backgrounds that they decide on can help shape the play style and the general thrust of the campaign. While some GMs will decide to take all of the player input and craft their own intricate worlds for them to explore, many more will set their adventures in the settings and kingdoms of established worlds.

In this chapter, we will explore some of the most famous fantasy realms alongside some stranger ones that never quite caught on. You'll see questions such as: What famous adventurers have already helped shape the world before your characters got on the scene, and what landmarks of wonder might they see during their escapades? Or what events have made life better or worse for the people living there?

Most games come with a baseline setting baked into the game unless they are a truly generic system. Some games manage to have all sorts of different settings that you can experience that will have aspects of many genres, such as horror or sci-fi, even while still being decidedly fantasy. Other games are deeply rooted in a single setting and fleshed out with all manner of amazing and intricate details. Whatever world your players happen to find themselves in, this chapter will test the knowledge of even the most lore-focused reader.

Total Possible Points: 57

1

When the Forgotten Realms setting needed to introduce the Dragonborn as a main playable species, they needed to come up with a place they had lived in up until now. Where were the Dragonborn hanging out until they were introduced?

A. Islands of the Utter South, an unexplored series of islands.
B. Abeir, a planet in a pocket dimension.
C. Shurrock, one of the Outer Planes.
D. They were always there, just off camera.

2

What continent in the Forgotten Realms was originally made to be an ancient East Asia setting but was then combined with the Realms in 1987?

A. Kara-Tur
B. Shou Lung

C. Malatra
D. Kozakura

1. B. Abeir, a planet in a pocket dimension. 2. A. Kara-Tur.

54

True or false?: The World of Greyhawk in *D&D* was originally envisioned as a parallel Earth with magic that would be called Oerth.

Critical Info

The early adventures Gary Gygax created for his friends in the Greyhawk setting included such memorable characters as Yrag ("Gary" spelled backward), Drawmij ("Jim Ward" spelled backward), and the god Zagyg ("Gygax" backward with the *X* replaced with a *Z*).

4

While Greyhawk was the first published setting for *Dungeons & Dragons*, it wasn't the first one to be developed. The first setting was created by Dave Arneson and predates the creation of the *D&D* rules. What is it?

5

Due to the harsh climate and even harsher brutality of the Dark Sun setting, there is a single class that isn't generally allowed in the setting. What can't you play as in the world of Athas?

6

The Greyhawk setting is home to famous mages that have spells named after them. Match the spell with the wizard that it is associated with.

A. **Black Tentacles**

B. **Floating Disc**

C. **Grasping Hand**

D. **Lucubration**

E. **Acid Arrow**

F. **Irresistible Dance**

G. **Mnemonic Enhancer**

H. **Instant Summons**

1. **Rary**

2. **Bigby**

3. **Evard**

4. **Drawmij**

5. **Otto**

6. **Tenser**

7. **Mordenkainen**

8. **Melf**

6. A. Black Tentacles & 3. Evard. B. Floating Disc & 6. Tenser. C. Grasping Hand & 2. Bigby. D. Lucubration & 7. Mordenkainen. E. Acid Arrow & 8. Melf. F. Irresistible Dance & 5. Otto. G. Mnemonic Enhancer & 1. Rary. H. Instant Summons & 4. Drawmij.

56

7

The planet of Krynn is home to the Dragonlance setting. This world was also the inspiration for many different fantasy novels. Which one of these was not one of the novels in the original Dragonlance Chronicles trilogy?

A. *Dragons of Autumn Twilight*

B. *Dragons of Winter Night*

C. *Dragons of Spring Dawning*

D. *Dragons of Summer Zenith*

8

True or false?: While similar to most standard *D&D* settings in many ways, Dragonlance replaced the standard Halflings with Kender, a group of thieving little people with no concept of personal property.

9

The Dark Sun setting is a departure from standard *D&D* in that it mixes a lot of post-apocalyptic tropes in with the fantasy ones. The planet is mostly wasteland with pockets of corrupt city-states run by brutal dictators known as what?

A. Wizard-Gods

B. Mage-Emperors

C. Sorcerer-Kings

D. Evoker-Princes

7. D. *Dragons of Summer Zenith*. 8. True. 9. C. Sorcerer-Kings.

57

10

One of the more recent additions to the *Dungeons & Dragons* setting list is that of Eberron. Great Houses provide all kinds of services using their Dragonmarks, sigils that appear on members of the house and provide magical power. There used to be thirteen marks, but one has since been lost. Which mark no longer exists?

A. The Mark of Finding

B. The Mark of Shadow

C. The Mark of Death

D. The Mark of Disappearing

11

Eberron introduced four new races for players to choose, with some being based on standard D&D creatures and others being entirely new. Which of these wasn't introduced for the first time in Eberron?

A. Changeling

B. Tiefling

C. Shifter

D. Warforged

12

True or false?: Most Dwarves in Pathfinder venerate the god Torag. The rest of the dwarven pantheon is just Torag's family like his wife, kids, and siblings.

10. C. The Mark of Death. 11. B. Tiefling. 12. False. There is also Droskar, the deity of the Duergar with no relation to Torag.

13

True or false?: The prevalence of high-level magic in Eberron means that most cities offer resurrection, and there is a magical teleportation network set up between the major capitals.

Critical Info

Magic is such a constant force in the world of Eberron that there is a continent-spanning "lightning rail" train system that provides high-speed transportation. The world also has standard air ships.

14

Speaking of the gods of Pathfinder, it turns out that even mere mortals can ascend to demigod status. All they need to do is pass the Test of the Starstone. While many have tried, only four have ever succeeded in getting to the Starstone. What was the reason Cayden Cailean took on the challenge?

A. He was seeking a cure for his father's illness.
B. He wanted to bring glory to his nation.
C. He wanted justice for his murdered friend.
D. He did it on a drunken bet.

13. False. The setting has focus on prevalent low-level magic such as magic streetlamps.
14. D. He did it on a drunken bet.

15

The show *Critical Role* has had a huge impact on the RPG space including getting the setting for their adventures turned into an officially published one. What is the name of their world?

16

In a bid to tie into their other properties more, Hasbro and Wizards of the Coast began to publish settings for D&D from the worlds of *Magic: The Gathering*. What plane allows PCs to be a Circle of Spores Druid with magic based on decay and regrowth?

A. Theros

B. Ravnica

C. Innistrad

D. Dominaria

17

The main setting of the *Pathfinder Roleplaying Game* has many lands that encompass all sorts of different tropes and real-world influences. The land of Numeria is a harsh land of windswept plains with rugged people that eke out their existence. It is also home to what strange inhabitants?

A. Holograms

B. Angels

C. Androids

D. Undead Bards

15. Exandria. 16. B. Ravnica. 17. C. Androids.

18

True or false?: In a setting grounded in myth, *Pendragon* allows you to play as a knight in the times of King Arthur. Rather than Goblins or Orcs, the main enemies you'll fight are probably Saxons.

19

Like most fantasy settings, the world of Pathfinder is loaded with magic and miracles. However, there is one place that exists where magic simply doesn't work and sometimes the laws of reality are damaged. Where is this wild and unpredictable area?

20

The world of *Hârn* was originally made as a system-agnostic fantasy setting that you could use for your RPG way back in 1983. Eventually, an entire game was developed specifically for players to delve into the world of *Hârn*. What was it called?

When it comes to the politics in Pathfinder, the different countries and regions all have their own codes and laws that they live by. What does the Royal Proclamation of the Draconic Banking in Taldor allow?

A. Red dragons can freely store their hoard in any government bank.

B. Bronze dragons can set up banks without paying taxes.

C. Copper dragons aren't allowed to borrow money from banks.

D. Debtors have one final chance to steal a dragon's hoard before going to prison.

22

The setting for *Ars Magica* is that of Mythic Europe. This Europe is geographically and politically almost identical to the actual Europe of the twelfth and thirteenth centuries, except the beliefs of the time are actually true. For example, there really were child-stealing fairies and crop-withering demons. Players generally alternate between being a magus (wizard) and a companion (wizard helper). What are the mundane peasants that are also technically playable known as?

A. Peons   **B.** Hermits   **C.** Grogs   **D.** Mercs

21. B. Bronze dragons can set up banks without paying taxes. 22. C. Grogs.

62

23

True or false?: The setting of Glorantha from the *RuneQuest* RPG did what many fantasy settings have done and included Elves and Dwarves, but changed them up a little to make them more original. The Elves are also known as Aldryami and are actually humanoid-shaped plant creatures.

24

Amber is well known for being the first diceless RPG, but it is also entirely based on The Chronicles of Amber universe by Roger Zelazny. The main assumption of the game is that the players will play as children of the main Elder Amberites from the books. If players want to populate the setting with entirely new Elder Amberites instead and play as them, that is known as what type of game?

A. Amethyst   **B.** Argent   **C.** Argyle   **D.** Paisley

Critical Info

The Chronicles of Amber offers another way to play the game if you don't like those other ideas. Players can instead set the game before the events of the book series using their own Amberites vying for the throne. This is a good option for those who want the freedom to entirely rewrite the history of the books while keeping the setting more or less intact.

25

Synnibarr is a game that has a setting that is so complicated, long, and weird that even doing a summary of it is impossible in this space. The setting has no shortage of absolutely wild monsters that players can encounter. Which one of these is an actual monster that exists in the setting?

A. A giant slug that vomits lava.
B. A flying grizzly bear with laser eyes.
C. A shark made of diamond.
D. A kangaroo that shoots lightning.

26

The world of Talislanta eschews the standard elf and dwarf from the selection of species. It doesn't even really have humans as much as several subsets of not-quite humans known as the Races of Man. Which one of these isn't one of the unique playable species?

A. Mogroth, sloth-like humanoids
B. Aeriad, a bird-like people
C. Kazman, small blue burrowers
D. Parthenians, metallic-skinned seafarers

25. B. A flying grizzly bear with laser eyes. 26. C. Kazman, small blue burrowers.

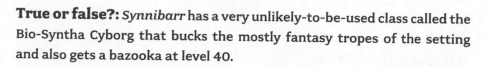

27

True or false?: *Synnibarr* has a very unlikely-to-be-used class called the Bio-Syntha Cyborg that bucks the mostly fantasy tropes of the setting and also gets a bazooka at level 40.

Critical Info

We know we said it would be impossible to summarize the setting of *Synnibarr*, but here's a small taste. The setting takes place on Mars fifty thousand years in the future, after a god's avatar (maybe Jesus?) hollowed it out. The Mars husk was then turned into a spaceship to take humanity elsewhere, as Earth was destroyed by evil gods. Of course, none of that has any bearing on play.

28

In the *Earthdawn* setting, players explore a post-apocalyptic fantasy as people are just starting to reclaim the surface. The struggles of the planet happened after a time of heightened magic that allowed monsters to invade the planet. What was the period where people hid in magical shelters to protect themselves known as?

A. The Scourge

B. The Age of Monsters

C. The Horror

D. The Event

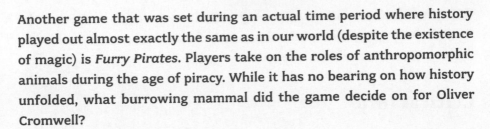

29

Another game that was set during an actual time period where history played out almost exactly the same as in our world (despite the existence of magic) is *Furry Pirates*. Players take on the roles of anthropomorphic animals during the age of piracy. While it has no bearing on how history unfolded, what burrowing mammal did the game decide on for Oliver Cromwell?

30

The *Mistborn Adventure Game* is an RPG based on the Mistborn series by Brandon Sanderson. In the world of Scadrial, magic is based on the use of various metals to accomplish various things. What metal would an allomancer use to increase their physical capabilities?

A. Steel **B.** Zinc **C.** Pewter **D.** Gold

Critical Info

Normally an allomancer in the *Mistborn* setting is capable of burning a single metal for its power. So someone who could burn tin in order to enhance their senses is known as a Tineye. The titular *Mistborn* are those who are capable of using any and all of the metals.

Fantasy games love to have their interesting non-human species. Many stick to the tried-and-true Tolkien races and maybe branch out a little. Others have some truly unique offerings. Match the unique species with the game it comes from.

A. Thri-Kreen,
four-armed bug people

1. *Empire of the Petal Throne*

B. Kharakhan,
twelve-foot, gray-skinned giants

2. *Numenera*

c. Calramites,
humanoids with tentacles for arms

3. *Earthdawn*

D. T'skrang,
semi-aquatic dino-people

4. *Talislanta*

E. Timinits,
various types of insect people

5. *Glorantha*

F. Chameleon Drake,
human/dragon hybrid

6. *D&D: Dark Sun*

G. Swamp Folk,
four-legged, round, and rubbery

7. *Synnibarr*

31. A. Thri-Kreen, four-armed bug people & 6. *D&D: Dark Sun.* B. Kharakhan, twelve-foot, gray-skinned giants & 4. *Talislanta.* C. Calramites, humanoids with tentacles for arms & 2. *Numenera.* D. T'skrang, semi-aquatic dino-people & 3. *Earthdawn.* E. Timinits, various types of insect people & 5. *Glorantha.* F. Chameleon Drake, human/dragon hybrid & 7. *Synnibarr.* G. Swamp Folk, four-legged, round, and rubbery & 1. *Empire of the Petal Throne.*

32

While still having the trappings and magic of most fantasy settings, *Blue Rose* has an interesting way for the ruling monarch of the Kingdom of Aldis to be chosen. How is the new king/queen chosen?

A. A week-long contest of craftsmanship
B. A magical deer picks somebody to rule
C. A child will be born with a birthmark of a crown
D. Democratically elected monarch

33

The RPG based on the series of novels about Elric of Melniboné was originally called *Stormbringer*, named after the magical sword that the titular hero wields. A 4th edition of the game substantially reworked the system, and it changed its name. What was it renamed after?

34

True or false?: Not content to merely come up with weird names for their various species, *Skyrealms of Jorune* makes up entire new words for things like "sword," which is now known as "condrij."

32. B. A magical deer picks somebody to rule. 33. *Elric! Dark Fantasy Roleplaying.* 34. False. Swords are just swords. Condrij is, however, the name for a mercenary.

68

35

Not every fantasy game needs to be rooted in the European idea of fantasy. In the *Legend of the Five Rings Roleplaying Game*, the game is set in a fantasy land of samurai and shugenja known as Rokugan. The various animal-themed clans have certain aspects or callings within the empire they are famous for. Match the clan with what they are known for.

A. Crab

B. Crane

C. Dragon

D. Lion

E. Mantis

F. Phoenix

G. Scorpion

H. Unicorn

1. Naval power

2. Cavalry

3. Physical strength

4. Deception

5. Magic

6. Duelists and Artisans

7. Military valor

8. Mysterious Monks

35. A. Crab & 3. Physical strength. B. Crane & 6. Duelists and Artisans. C. Dragon & 8. Mysterious Monks. D. Lion & 7. Military valor. E. Mantis & 1. Naval power. F. Phoenix & 5. Magic. G. Scorpion & 4. Deception. H. Unicorn & 2. Cavalry.

36

A recently published game and indie darling, *Mörk Borg* has a fantasy setting seen through the lens of a death metal album cover. The bleak, apocalyptic landscape is full of danger, and every day the GM rolls to see if a Misery occurs. What happens when all the listed Miseries have been read?

37

Known as a fantasy heartbreaker, the game *Fifth Cycle* has players make characters in a world where magic got out of control and was eventually banned. The magic of this world is only just now being allowed again, and players who are magic wielders are also known as what?

A. Merchants sent out to gather exotic wares.

B. Archaeologists sent out to explore ancient ruins.

C. Peacekeepers sent out to ensure magic isn't abused.

D. Adventurers sent out to kill some goblins.

36. The world ends. 37. B. Archaeologists sent out to explore ancient ruins.

70

38

True or false?: While the Satanic Panic caused some to think of RPGs as tools of the devil, *DragonRaid* was a game that was specifically made to teach kids about Christian values and biblical knowledge.

39

Set in a fantasy/steampunk hybrid setting, the *Iron Kingdoms* RPG has a world of magic that has undergone an industrial revolution. Now the warcasters can link their minds with powerful mechanical constructs known as what?

40

What destructive event in the Forgotten Realms, also known as the Blue Breath of Change, was thought to have been caused by the death of Mystra, the goddess of magic?

4

SPOOKY
SANITY SAVES

Questions about Horror RPGs from *All Flesh Must Be Eaten* to *Vampire: The Masquerade*

Role-playing games have been trying to present the horrific and the frightful for as long as they've been around. Whether that means fighting off hordes of the undead as a cleric or being one of the undead that prowls the streets, the trappings and tropes of the horror genre are deeply ingrained in RPGs. Some games, however, make their entire storylines and settings horror-based. From the deeply disturbing to the morose and gothic, the games in this chapter focus on the creepy crawlies that keep us up at night. That said, there are all kinds of ways to introduce the horror genre and the ways in which players interact with it. Some RPGs want you to be a powerless mortal facing truly unknowable monsters from beyond that you can only hope to delay, rather than stop them entirely. Other games put you in the role of a monster, stalking your prey at night and trying to avoid being found out by those that would hunt you for what you are.

Whichever approach the game takes, all the RPGs mentioned in this chapter will have that ghoulish touch. Maybe it's what the game is about, or maybe the game just has some rules for how to deal with those things if (and when) they show up. Get ready to test your RPG knowledge of the macabre with this terrifying trivia.

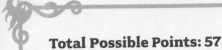

Total Possible Points: 57

1

Often considered the biggest name in horror RPGs, *Vampire: The Masquerade* has players take on the role of a vampire in a hidden society with different clans that all have their own secret powers and agendas. Which of these is not a clan that has been introduced in the game?

A. Ravnos

B. Salubri

C. Hecata

D. Maldovian

2

Vampiric legend Dracula actually exists within the world of *Vampire: The Masquerade*, which is an oddity given that the entire point of the titular masquerade is that humans don't find out about vampires. What clan embraced the superstar vampire?

A. Lesombra

B. Ventrue

C. Tzimisce

D. Toreador

1. D. Maldovian 2. C. Tzimisce.

3

True or false?: Cthulhu is a terrifying Outer God that would surely spell doom for all of humanity should a group of investigators somehow fail to stop him from being awakened.

4

Final question about *Vampire: The Masquerade* clans, we swear. One of the main clans is named after a famous vampire movie. Or we suppose, in universe, the movie would be named after the vampire clan? Anyway, what is the name of these monstrous vampires?

5

True or false?: *Don't Look Back: Terror is Never Far Behind* was a horror game about investigating supernatural occurrences that used a dice pool that was calculated using the absolute value of a character's bonuses or penalties.

Critical Info

The absolute value of a number is the distance a number is away from 0. So 3 and –3 would both have an absolute value of 3. This is generally not something you usually need to know in order to play an RPG, but you should never let something like that stop you when designing a game.

3. False. Cthulhu is a Great Old One. 4. Nosferatu. 5. True.

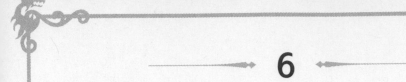

6

When dealing with something truly terrifying in the game *Rifts*, a monster would have its own separate attribute that would be the roll for avoiding being scared. This attribute is known as what?

A. Horror Factor

B. Terror Rating

C. Spooky Score

D. Monster Machination

7

"The Call of Cthulhu" is a popular short story that inspired the creation of the horror RPG *Call of Cthulhu*. Who was the author of the original short story?

8

A werewolf in the White Wolf game *Werewolf: The Apocalypse* is more of an eco-terrorist than a mindless beast that feasts on the unwary. This werewolf group is constantly fighting a never-ending war against the forces of what godlike spirit?

A. The Wulf

B. The Wyrm

C. The Waker

D. The Wyvern

9

RPG publisher White Wolf is famous for having a lot of games that follow the naming convention of "Something: The Descriptor"—for example, *Vampire: The Masquerade* and *Werewolf: The Apocalypse*. Match up the following to form each game's complete title.

A. *Vampire*

B. *Werewolf*

C. *Mage*

D. *Changeling*

E. *Promethean*

F. *Wraith*

G. *Mummy*

H. *Demon*

1. *The Ascension*

2. *The Created*

3. *The Oblivion*

4. *The Requiem*

5. *The Forsaken*

6. *The Fallen*

7. *The Resurrection*

8. *The Dreaming*

9. A. Vampire & 4. The Requiem. B. Werewolf & 5. The Forsaken. C. Mage & 1. The Ascension. D. Changeling & 8. The Dreaming. E. Promethean & 2. The Created. F. Wraith & 3. The Oblivion. G. Mummy & 7. The Resurrection. H. Demon & 6. The Fallen.

10

Call of Cthulhu can take place at any point in time and be set wherever the players like, but the general setting for the game, at least timewise, is a specific decade. When is the default setting for the game?

11

True or false?: When you want to act out being a vampire in a LARP, you can continue *The Masquerade* with the *Mind's Eye Theater* rules and settle disputes with a game of Rock, Paper, Scissors instead of dice.

12

Ravenloft is a campaign setting for *Dungeons & Dragons* where all the things that go bump in the night are in control and the populace lives in fear. It is a pocket dimension that is outside the Material Plane and is also known as what?

A. The Plane of Terror

C. The Quasiplane of Horror

B. The Demiplane of Dread

D. The Spooky Place

13

Ravenloft is split into many different domains, each of them ruled over by a Darklord that twists the area to suit their foul whims. The most famous of these Darklords is the vampire ruler of the Strahd von Zarovich, who serves as the poster boy for the setting. What is the name of the domain that Strahd rules over?

A. Transylvarria

B. Romeria

C. Barovia

D. The Spooky Place

14

True or false?: One of the famous places that an investigator might go looking for information in a *Call of Cthulhu* game is the Arkham University located in the fictional town of Miskatonic, Massachusetts.

15

Mind Flayers in *D&D* are scary enough on their own given their tentacled faces and penchant for eating brains, but when one of them gets to be magically undead, they can be truly horrific. What is the name of an undead Mind Flayer?

A. Vampiric Illithid

B. Alhoon

C. Illithilich

D. All of the above

13. C. Barovia. 14. False. It's Miskatonic University in the city of Arkham. 15. D. All of the above.

16

The White Wolf horror games all technically take place in the same universe and could, ostensibly, interact with each other. What is the umbrella term for the setting that all of these games exist in?

17

White Wolf is the publisher name that the company uses for the vast majority of their game releases, but they also have an imprint name that they use to release "mature" content with adult themes. What is the name of the imprint?

- **A.** Black Dog
- **B.** Red Claw
- **C.** Brown Bear
- **D.** Blue Barracuda

Critical Info

The mature imprint for White Wolf had some seriously different ideas on what "mature" meant. They had games ranging from the swearing and general edgy toilet humor of something like *Human Occupied Landfill* to the somber look at the ghosts of the Holocaust in *Charnel Houses of Europe: The Shoah*.

18

True or false?: In *The World of Tales from the Crypt* RPG, the players are trapped in different scary dimensions and must each find the Crypt Keeper to get out.

19

The Red Wizards of Thay are a powerful group of magic users in the Forgotten Realms of *D&D*. Their kingdom was turned into a realm of the undead with liches, vampires, and other undead casters in power due to the leadership of what wizard?

A. Maligor

B. Rath Modar

C. Szass Tam

D. Rotface

20

While the Darklords of Ravenloft rule their domains with an iron fist and have near absolute power within them, they are also prisoners that cannot go beyond the mists that border their kingdoms. Only one of the Darklords has managed to escape their kingdom and terrorizes the rest of the *D&D* universe. Who is it?

A. Lord Soth

B. Count Strahd

C. Baroness Obour

D. Captain Monette

18. False. The Crypt Keeper is the one keeping the players in the horror stories. 19. C. Szass Tam. 20. A. Lord Soth.

21

Monsterhearts is a game that leans into being a teenager in high school but also probably a monster. We say "probably" because you could also just be Human, but then again, isn't Man the real monster? Anyway, match up the playbook with one of the moves that they can start with.

A. The Chosen

B. The Fae

C. The Ghost

D. The Ghoul

E. The Infernal

F. The Mortal

G. The Vampire

H. The Werewolf

1. The Hunger

2. True Love

3. Cold as Ice

4. Creep

5. Final Showdown

6. Scent of Blood

7. Soul Debt

8. The Constant Bargain

21. A. The Chosen & 5. Final Showdown. B. The Fae & 8. The Constant Bargain. C. The Ghost & 4. Creep. D. The Ghoul & 1. The Hunger. E. The Infernal & 7. Soul Debt. F. The Mortal & 2. True Love. G. The Vampire & 3. Cold as Ice. H. The Werewolf & 6. Scent of Blood.

Critical Info

Monsterhearts is a game about discovery and how messy and weird it is growing up and figuring out who you actually are. It has a move to Turn Someone On with no restrictions because you never know who or what you might find attractive, and grappling with that is part of it. Being a kid is weird. Even if you aren't a vampire.

22

The *Alien* RPG allows players to make characters that are representative of the types of people that were in the Alien movies, including kids. What is not included as one of the signature items you can start the game with as a kid?

A. Lunchbox covered in stickers
B. Loose assortment of trading cards
C. Favorite doll or action figure
D. Bracelet made by older sibling

23

True or false?: In the *Buffy the Vampire Slayer Roleplaying Game*, the players act as supporting heroes while the GM takes on the role of the Slayer.

22. B. Loose assortment of trading cards. 23. False. Slayer is just another class you can play in the game.

24

In the zombie game *All Flesh Must Be Eaten*, there are a number of pre-generated archetypes that a player can choose from if they want to jump right into the game and start playing. Which one of these is an actual archetype that is available?

A. Video Store Clerk

B. Pizza Delivery Person

C. Bank Teller

D. Dog Catcher

25

True or false?: *All Flesh Must Be Eaten* allows for the game to be run without dice. You can replace the dice with playing cards, or opt to use no randomization at all.

26

Outbreak: Undead has a quiz system that players can fill out in order to automatically assess what their stats in the game might be in order to play as themselves during a zombie apocalypse. What does the game call this system?

A. FLEM-AI

B. PUKE-AI

C. CHUM-AI

D. SPEW-AI

27

In the game *Spookshow*, ghosts are real, but nobody knows about their existence or believes that they are real except for certain government agencies. What job do these agencies give to the ectoplasmic entities?

28

In the *Kult* RPG, you can play all types of horrific scenarios, from fending off waves of monsters to investigating the occult mysteries of the world. Within the game, nothing is as it seems. Which one of these is a true fact about the world of *Kult*?

A. Jesus is still around and has started a cult of Ascension.
B. All cops work for the metaphysical jailers of our reality.
C. Humans are immortal superbeings, they just don't know it yet.
D. All of the above

29

True or false?: *The Whispering Vault* is a game where players play as monstrous supernatural hunters tracking down evil entities. The hunters' goal is to throw the rogue beings back into the titular Whispering Vault for safekeeping.

The Cthulhu Mythos has spread into different games and systems. You can't turn a corner in the RPG world without running into some sort of horror from beyond time and space. Match up the horror RPG with the game system it uses.

A. *Trail of Cthulhu*

B. *Cthulhu Dark*

C. *Cthulhu Invictus*

D. *Cohors Cthulhu*

E. *Realms of Cthulhu*

F. *CthulhuPunk*

G. *CthulhuTech*

H. *tremulus*

1. **Modiphius 2d20**

2. **Savage Worlds**

3. **GURPS**

4. **Gumshoe**

5. **Powered by the Apocalypse**

6. **Cthulhu Dark**

7. **Framewerk**

8. **Basic Role-Playing**

30. A. *Trail of Cthulhu* & 4. Gumshoe. B. *Cthulhu Dark* & 6. Cthulhu Dark. C. *Cthulhu Invictus* & 8. Basic Role-Playing. D. *Cohors Cthulhu* & 1. Modiphius 2d20. E. *Realms of Cthulhu* & 2. Savage Worlds. F. *CthulhuPunk* & 3. GURPS. G. *CthulhuTech* & 7. Framewerk. H. *tremulus* & 5. Powered by the Apocalypse.

86

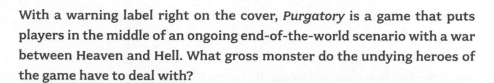

31

With a warning label right on the cover, *Purgatory* is a game that puts players in the middle of an ongoing end-of-the-world scenario with a war between Heaven and Hell. What gross monster do the undying heroes of the game have to deal with?

A. Fart Demons

B. Rectal Slugs

C. Poop Crickets

D. Cavity Creeps

32

Palladium published a game about people that became aware that the world was infiltrated by shapeshifting monsters from another dimension. These people then became monstrous themselves in order to combat them. Originally titled *Nightspawn*, it was later changed after legal threats. What did the game change its name to?

Critical Info

The legal threats were issued by Todd McFarlane, creator of the Spawn comic book series, because of the similarity in name. Oddly, it wasn't Clive Barker, creator of the film *Nightbreed*, which the game is very clearly referencing in both the themes and title.

31. B. Rectal Slugs. 32. *Nightbane*.

33

Palladium published a game about people that realized supernatural monsters exist and, yes, we're talking about an entirely different game. The game is *Beyond the Supernatural*, and in the game, players are paranormal investigators that will often die in a stiff breeze. Those with psychic powers could use their ISP to do amazing feats, such as not being as cold. What does ISP stand for?

34

True or false?: *NightLife* is a game where the players play iconic horror-type creatures like vampires, werewolves, and ghosts. Interestingly, included in the list of playable supernatural creatures is a nature spirit called the Inuit, which is named after a group of real Indigenous people.

35

True or false?: *Cthulhu Live* gives the rules and structure for running a LARP in the world of the Cthulhu Mythos. In order to make things as spooky as possible, it also comes with detailed instructions on making tentacles out of foam rubber and bedsheets.

36

Scared Stiff is a horror RPG that leans more heavily into the schlocky types of horror than the truly terrifying ones. It uses the jokey RPG-13 B-Movie Game System and is full of classic "drive-in" type horror. Even the GM gets their own fun title. What is it?

A. Budget Director

B. Alien Overlord

C. Evil Mastermind

D. Grave Master

37

The game *Chill* is another game where the world is simultaneously plagued by monsters and yet nobody believes in them. There is a secret society of believers, however, that keep the common man safe from the worst parts of the supernatural. What is the name for that secret society?

A. HELP

B. SAVE

C. GONE

D. NUTS

38

There were numerous supplements over the two editions for the game *Chill*, and they covered all sorts of specific horror scenarios. There were supplement books on Lycanthropes and Apparitions, but there was also an entire book on what real world religion?

36. C. Evil Mastermind 37. B. SAVE. 38. Voodoo.

39

True or false?: In a game that attempted to make a mind-bending experience for the players, *Psychosis* uses a deck of standard playing cards to adjudicate settings where reality is constantly shifting and the players have to figure out what is actually going on.

40

True or false?: In the *Horror Adventures* supplement for *Pathfinder*, the characters do not have merely a single Sanity Score like *Call of Cthulhu*. Instead, they have four: Sanity Score, Sanity Threshold, Sanity Edge, and Sanity Defense.

41

In a wholly contained setting outside the standard White Wolf stuff, there is a company that employs ghosts and people that can astral project to solve supernatural problems. What Greek hero is this setting and company named after?

39. False. The game uses tarot cards. 40. False. There is no Sanity Defense. 41. Orpheus.

42

The idea that the people you know have been replaced by imposters is featured in the game *Exquisite Replicas*, and only a few people can actually see the replacements for what they are. What exactly is it that is replacing these people?

- **A.** Aliens from outer space
- **B.** Government clones
- **C.** Invaders from another dimension
- **D.** Robotic artificial intelligence

Critical Info

The delusion that the people you know and love have actually been replaced by look-alikes is a real thing. It's known as Capgras syndrome and can also make the sufferer believe that a pet or even an inanimate object has been replaced by an exact duplicate.

42. C. Invaders from another dimension.

5

LICENSED
CREATIONS

Questions about the Best and Wildest Licensed Games, from *Star Wars* to *Cap'n Crunch*

There is a rich tradition of role-playing game properties making the transition from pen and paper to film and television, though the road to today's popular offerings such as *Dungeons & Dragons: Honor Among Thieves* and *Vox Machina* has been paved with...how do we put this delicately...garbage that flies won't land on. The first few RPG films weren't licensed by any particular RPG, but rather were scary films about the nebulous threats represented by unspecified games. They were a mélange of fearmongering wrought by pearl-clutching fundamentalists and filmmakers looking to sensationalize the hot new American scare. As the panic subsided, we were left with a few isolated oddities on TV until 2000, when the first *Dungeons & Dragons* movie arrived, to the adulation and applause of very, very few. Thankfully, it's been mostly up since then.

Today's media landscape is filled with all manner of shows pulled directly from popular RPGs, inspired by those RPGs, or merely paying some homage to them. *Stranger Things* of course is infused with the essence of classing dungeon-crawling D&D and even borrows names of the hideous monsters of those game worlds, while popular actual-play podcasts such as *The Adventure Zone* and *Critical Role* have become so large and well liked that they've become empires of their own, producing their own RPGs, comics, and even cartoons. While it's been largely *Dungeons & Dragons* on every bit of available branding, a few products such as *Cyberpunk Edgerunners* have begun to show the wonders of other RPGs to the public at large as well.

1

Being a gaming nerd has never been more popular, even among Hollywood celebrities, with such names as Stephen Colbert, Jon Favreau, Deborah Ann Woll, and Joseph Gordon-Levitt happily playing and discussing their favorite games in interviews and shows. However, one celebrity, Vin Diesel, has taken this farther than most, having actually turned one of his childhood *D&D* characters into a movie! What movie was it?

A. Riddick

B. The Last Witch Hunter

C. Barbarian King

D. Dark Elf Warlock: The Movie

2

Boxed murder mystery games, as much puzzle as live-action RPG, have been popular in game stores since the board game Cluedo was released in 1948. Occasionally, these games will pop up in movies or television. What was the name of the murder mystery box game played on *The Office* season 6 episode, "Murder"?

1. B. The Last Witch Hunter. 2. Belles, Bourbon, and Bullets.

94

There's a famous anti-*D&D* Chick tract (a series of moralizing evangelical comic strips published by independent artist Jack Chick beginning in 1964) implying that the players use actual spells on their families, and introducing the usual cyberspace movie convention "If you die in the game, you die in real life!" The tract is called *Dark Dungeons*, but what is the name of the thief that was declared dead and, for further fun, the name of their player?

A. Black Leaf and Marcie
B. Shendranalaine and Alison
C. Backstabbitha and Jane
D. Doug the Rogue and Doug

Critical Info

Dark Dungeons was so infamous in gaming and nerd circles as a silly bit of reactionary scaremongering that it was acted out/heavily parodied in a 2014 film of the same name. All the scenes from the original tract are still present. However, the filmmakers worked overtime to ensure their perspective stood in stark contrast to the original comic, adding queer themes, cool action montages, and the skewering of other stodgy prejudicial figures from RPG history. (Lovecraft's Chthonic entities were featured heavily, as well as the steam tunnels of *Mazes and Monsters* fame.) The film premiered at gaming convention GenCon in 2014 and has become a bit of a cult classic since then.

4

Connect these notable examples of named fantasy weaponry to the movie or TV show hero that most famously wields them.

A. Longclaw

B. The Glaive

C. The Sword of Omens

D. Brisingr

E. The Atlantean Sword

F. Ivory Dragon Katana

G. Frostmourne

H. Sunsword

1. Eragon, *Eragon*

2. Thundarr, *Thundarr the Barbarian*

3. Connor MacLeod, *Highlander*

4. Lion-O, *Thundercats*

5. Arthas Menethil, *World of Warcraft*

6. Colwyn, *Krull*

7. Jon Snow, *Game of Thrones*

8. Conan, *Conan the Barbarian*

4. A. Longclaw & 7. Jon Snow, *Game of Thrones*. B. The Glaive & 6. Colwyn, *Krull*. C. The Sword of Omens & 4. Lion-O, *Thundercats*. D. Brisingr & 1. Eragon, *Eragon*. E. The Atlantean Sword & 8. Conan, *Conan the Barbarian*. F. Ivory Dragon Katana & 3. Connor MacLeod, *Highlander*. G. Frostmourne & 5. Arthas Menethil, *World of Warcraft* H. Sunsword & 2. Thundarr, *Thundarr the Barbarian*.

5

True or false?: In 2003, Palladium Games announced that the *Rifts* RPG had been optioned for a film by Walt Disney Pictures, with Jerry Bruckheimer attached to direct.

6

During the nineties, White Wolf and their flagship game *Vampire: The Masquerade* seemed unstoppable, offering real competition to D&D in numbers sold and tables playing the game at conventions, game stores, and at home—and spawning enormous networks of players both at tables and in live-action LARP gatherings. White Wolf didn't stop there though, foraying into mainstream media as they went. What was the name of the TV show based on *Vampire: The Masquerade* (which only lasted one season)?

- **A.** *Vampire: The Eternal Dance*
- **B.** *Buffy the Vampire Slayer*
- **C.** *Kindred: The Embraced*
- **D.** *That's My Tzimisce!*

7

What was the name of the mystical weapon sought after by the *South Park* gang when they tried to save *World of Warcraft* from the dread Alliance griefer?

5. True. 6. C. *Kindred: The Embraced.* 7. *The Sword of a Thousand Truths.*

Not content to stop at (honestly fairly bad) TV shows, White Wolf would even lend their name and license to a professional wrestler performing in the WWF (as it was known at the time)! What vampiric name would the over-the-top wrestler David Heath adopt as his ring persona?

A. The Toreador

B. Bone Gnawer

C. Gangrel

D. Promethean: The Created Man

Critical Info

After the nineties, White Wolf continued finding innovative ways to publicize their brand. While wrestlers and TV shows seemed like elements of the past, they still found some unexpected avenues to explore, such as the 2018 release of the *Vampire: The Masquerade* Book Makeup Palette, featuring a collection of lip shades designed specifically to highlight and identify the vampire clans associated with the 5th edition of *Vampire: The Masquerade*, including Nosferatu Green and Malkavian Clan Blue lipsticks. The selection was produced in collaboration with Belladonna's Cupboard, a makeup company that primarily worked in horror films and haunted houses/tours. Truly a match to die for.

True or false?: In 1993, TSR would release *Dragonstrike,* a board game/RPG hybrid designed to introduce new players to *D&D* via a VHS tape featuring actors in full *D&D* costume battling monsters and explaining the mechanics of their character classes.

True or false?: *DragonStrike* would go on to have a successful published sequel in the follow-up game *Wildspace,* in which the same cast would journey into the Spelljammer space setting of *Dungeons & Dragons.*

Debuting in 1983, the *Dungeons & Dragons* cartoon series presented a world of magic and danger, faced by a collection of (animated) real-world kids that were mysteriously transported to the famous fantasy game. The kids were menaced by all manner of terrifying creatures, but most deadly of all was the show's big bad. What was this foul fiend's name?

A. Venger

B. The Necromancer

C. Tarantulex

D. Yahmo Bethere

9. True. 10. False. While some pilot footage was shot for a planned sequel to feature the Spelljammer campaign setting, it was canceled prior to completion. 11. A. Venger.

12

In the 2000 film *Dungeons & Dragons*, the party must briefly contend with the leader of a bizarre local Thieves' Guild in order to retrieve an artifact. This leader is played by *Rocky Horror* writer and actor Richard O'Brien, but what was his name?

Critical Info

As his role in the film was to force the hero to navigate a deadly maze, the casting of O'Brien was likely a reference to his 1990–1993 gig as host of the game show *The Crystal Maze*. In this show, teams would compete in a variety of challenges to attain large Swarovski crystal orbs referred to as time crystals. The show was said to have similarities to *Dungeons & Dragons*, with O'Brien serving as a DM that observed and commented on contestants throughout their challenges. The show has seen several revivals, most recently with host Richard Ayoade that ended in 2020, and even an American spinoff by Nickelodeon in 2020.

13

True or false?: The third live-action film to feature the *Dungeons & Dragons* name was a Syfy original released in 2012 named *Dungeons & Dragons: The Book of Exalted Deeds*.

12. Xilus. 13. False. It was actually a British direct-to-DVD film titled *Dungeons & Dragons: The Book of Vile Darkness*, though it did premier in the US on Syfy.

14

Dungeons & Dragons was never content to stop with just one attempt to move into the media landscape and would eventually license their names to several films, starting with a Hollywood production distributed by New Line Cinema. It featured a deadly villain with a plan to conquer the land of Izmer by gaining control of all the red dragons in it (or something). What was his name?

A. High Lord Krantz

B. Profion

C. Bortrus

D. Ouroboros

15

True or false?: Both *Buffy the Vampire Slayer* and the spinoff series *Angel* featured episodes with *Dungeons & Dragons* or a facsimile being referred to or played in the background. Plus, both featured the weird notion that Dungeon Masters always wear a special cape that denotes their position.

16

What online show, created by Joshua "Jovenshire" Ovenshire, cocreator of Smosh Games, featured live puppets acting out the *D&D* adventures of a table of real players?

14. B. Profion. 15. True. 16. Stuff of Legends.

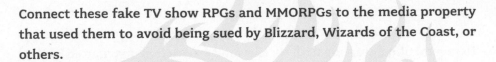

Connect these fake TV show RPGs and MMORPGs to the media property that used them to avoid being sued by Blizzard, Wizards of the Coast, or others.

A. Dragon Scuffle

B. Monsters and Mazes

C. Gryphons and Gargoyles

D. Moondoor

E. Dungeons, Dungeons, and More Dungeons

F. Dwarflord: The Conquest

G. Crypts and Creatures

H. Goblins and Grottos

1. *Riverdale*

2. *American Dad*

3. *Scooby-Doo! Mystery Incorporated*

4. *Gravity Falls*

5. *Dexter's Laboratory*

6. *Craig of the Creek*

7. *Lizzie McGuire*

8. *Supernatural*

17. A. Dragon Scuffle & 2. *American Dad.* B. Monsters and Mazes & 5. *Dexter's Laboratory.* C. Gryphons and Gargoyles & 1. *Riverdale.* D. Moondoor & 8. *Supernatural.* E. Dungeons, Dungeons and More Dungeons & 4. *Gravity Falls.* F. Dwarflord: The Conquest & 7. *Lizzie McGuire.* G. Crypts and Creatures & 3. *Scooby-Doo! Mystery Incorporated.* H. Goblins and Grottos & 6. *Craig of the Creek.*

18

What character class would best describe the character played by Marlon Wayans in the 2000 film *Dungeons & Dragons*? For a few hints and reminders, his name was Snails, he was the comic relief character (along with the dwarf, we suppose), he was afraid of everything, and he died in the movie.

A. Bard

B. Thief or Rogue

C. Monk

D. Some sort of Battle Clown

19

After the first *D&D* movie was a flop (who could have guessed it would be, other than anyone who has ever seen it), Wizards of the Coast didn't stop trying. They dusted themselves off and kept licensing their name to increasingly cheap movies. The second movie featured only one returning character from the first film (the dread sorcerer and second in command from the original, Damodar) and was largely about stopping him from destroying the world with a much more budget-friendly single black dragon. What was the name of this film?

A. *Dungeons & Dragons: The Sorcerer Returns*

B. *Dungeons & Dragons 2*

C. *Dungeons & Dragons: Wrath of the Dragon God*

D. *D&D2: The Mighty Ducks*

18. B. Thief or Rogue. 19. C. Dungeons & Dragons: Wrath of the Dragon God.

103

20

Which *Dragonlance* novel was made into an animated movie in 2008?

21

True or false?: The first published *D&D* comic books were a Spanish-language adaptation of the 1983 cartoon *Dungeon & Dragons*, known as *Dragones y Mazmorras*, published by Planeta DeAgostini.

22

The 2023 *D&D* film features a brief cameo from what other *D&D* media property, seen for just a moment during a climactic scene of gladiatorial maze survival near the end of the film?

- **A.** Strongheart and Warduke
- **B.** Stanley the Troll, from *A Troll in Central Park*
- **C.** Alias of the Azure Bonds and her Saurial Paladin associate Dragonbait
- **D.** The main cast of the *D&D* cartoon show from 1983

20. *Dragons of Autumn Twilight.* 21. True. 22. D. The main cast of the *D&D* cartoon show from 1983.

104

23

In the 2023 film *Dungeons & Dragons: Honor Among Thieves*, a young Tiefling Druid named Doric briefly transforms into a massive creature known as an Owlbear, a magical combination of two predatory animals (you'll never guess which) that is famous in *D&D* history and is one of the few monsters actually trademarked by Wizards of the Coast. This transformation sequence was in the first trailer for the film and caused a bit of online controversy. Why was the scene the cause of nerdy online arguments?

A. By default rules, Druids can only shapeshift into Beasts, and Owlbears are Monstrosities.

B. Doric was clearly too low level for a transformation of the Archdruid levels.

C. An Owlbear, being composed of two creatures, would require two shapeshifting charges, which she would not have after also transforming into a deer earlier in the scene.

D. Women cannot have cool abilities; the Internet hates that.

Critical Info

Wizards of the Coast did eventually acknowledge the concerns regarding Doric and her shapeshifting, whatever they might have been. (You can't find the answer in this sidebar!) They simply reiterated that the answer was already present in the core rules of the game, and that any rule the DM doesn't like, they are free to change. It is, after all, their table, their game, and their rules. So whatever the book said Doric theoretically wasn't allowed to do, the DM (here we suppose represented by screenwriters and/or directors) just said she was. So there.

23. A. By default rules, Druids can only shapeshift into Beasts, and Owlbears are Monstrosities.

24

What is the title of the fifth-season *Community* episode that served as a sequel of sorts to the second-season episode "Advanced Dungeons & Dragons?"

25

True or false?: Chris Pine's character in the 2023 film *Dungeons & Dragons: Honor Among Thieves* was a bard named Edgin Darvis, and as a bard, he wields short swords and rapiers.

26

In the *Star Trek: Deep Space Nine* episode "Move Along Home," Quark's bar is visited by a species called the Wadi, who force the Ferengi bar owner to play a game that uses the crew of the space station as pawns. What was the name of this game?

24. "Advanced Advanced Dungeons & Dragons". 25. False. Edgin wielded no weapons at all throughout the film, largely choosing to stand back and watch his more capable companions fight, or hit people with a musical instrument. 26. Chula.

27

In 2003, Wizards of the Coast released an entire CGI movie called *Scourge of Worlds: A Dungeons & Dragons Adventure*, in which a small group of heroes composed of the "iconic" representation characters from the 3.0 and 3.5 editions of *Dungeons & Dragons* (Regdar, Mialee, and Lidda) try to prevent the end of an already blighted and dying world. What was unique about this rare and unusual film?

A. Instead of the characters speaking in their own voices, the entire film is narrated as if played by a group of friends at a game night table.

B. The entire film is a choose-your-own-adventure—style decision tree, with multiple possible endings and stories.

C. The setting switches at various points through several of *D&D*'s iconic campaign worlds, including Ravenloft, Spelljammer, and Greyhawk.

D. Character actions are so true to the *D&D* game that you can see dice rolls occurring in a small inset box in the corner of the screen as the action plays out.

28

True or false?: Julian Luna, colead of the vampire television show *Kindred: The Embraced* was a member of the Brujah clan.

27. B. The entire film is a choose-your-own-adventure style decision tree, with multiple possible endings and stories. 28. False. Julian was actually a member of the Ventrue clan.

Hit Netflix TV show *Stranger Things* uses *D&D* as a resource for the themes and intent behind the various supernatural interplanar beasties that routinely plague the gang from Hawkins. Over the course of the show, they have referenced a number of monsters, gods, and things that are vaguely in between those categories as the titles given to each seasonal big bad. Which creature listed below has not yet been a big bad on *Stranger Things*?

A. Mind Flayer

B. Displacer Beast

C. Vecna

D. Demogorgon

What were the names of the characters played by the young boys of *Stranger Things* in their first *D&D* campaign (in 1983) depicted in the series?

A. Anomen, Mazzy, Cerngar, and Minsc

B. Tayr, Will the Wise, Sundar the Bold, and Nog

C. Alkurah, Verdence, Verity, and Lassiter the Brave

D. Bob the Dwarf, Spock the Elf, Arion, and Lucas

29. B. Displacer Beast. 30. B. Tayr, Will the Wise, Sundar the Bold, and Nog.

108

31

On *Stranger Things,* the main cast's characters would eventually be joined by a new one played by Lucas's little sister Erica, a half-elf rogue named:

32

True or false?: Outlandish brightly clad WWF wrestling character Max Moon was originally based on the FASA cyberpunk RPG *Shadowrun.*

33

The MMO that took over the world of the near future in *Ready Player One* (both in the book and the film adaptation) was an active hub of gaming, dating, socializing, business, and even schooling, a vast and sprawling game full of classic video game references, nightclubs, and mysterious secrets. What was it actually called though?

A. Oasis

B. The Digital Vista

C. Second Life

D. Boomer References Online

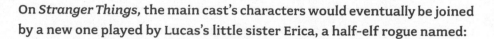

31. Lady Applejack. 32. False. Max Moon, portrayed by wrestler Paul Diamond, was not based on any RPG, but rather was just meant to be a wrestler from outer space. 33. A. Oasis.

34

The central character of R.A. Salvatore's Dungeons & Dragons novels is a Drow Ranger named Drizzt Do'Urden. What is the name of his traveling companion, an onyx statue of a panther that comes to life?

35

Within R.A. Salvatore's D&D novels, what fictional city in the world of Forgotten Realms did Drizzt Do'Urden originally hail from?

36

Cyd Sherman, played by Felicia Day, is at the heart of the web series *The Guild*, which focuses on the titular guild, the Knights of Good, and their daily interactions and adventures in their online game, *The Game*. What is her online avatar's name?

A. Cydthia Bloodmantle
B. Mistweaver

C. Codex
D. Kinga Forrester

37

Futuristic comedy cartoon *Futurama* featured which famous RPG designer as a member of Al Gore's Vice Presidential Action Rangers?

38

True or false?: *Darkest Dungeons* (the movie) featured not only the plot of the original Chick tract on which it was based, but also a foul plot to summon dread Cthulhu.

39

Complete the title of this movie, in which a LARP goes terribly wrong as the players accidentally conjure up a real demon from Hell that wreaks havoc on the players: *Knights of___:*

In the 1982 made-for-TV movie *Mazes and Monsters*, the lead character Robbie Wheeling (Tom Hanks) falls victim to the "perils of gaming," which results in him disassociating when facing his family fighting and the disappearance of his older brother. He begins to believe he is his character and vanishes from his college, leading the other members of his gaming group to eventually find him where and doing what?

A. Preparing to leap off the south tower observation deck of the World Trade Center.

B. Fiercely attacking a dragon statue at a miniature golf course with a sharpened putter.

C. Attempting to exorcize a demon from a figure skating child at an ice rink.

D. Preparing to battle a "purple worm," which was actually an oncoming NYC subway train.

Critical Info

Mazes and Monsters was based on a 1981 book of the same name written by novelist Rona Jaffe, which itself was largely sensationalized and based on inaccurate newspaper stories about the disappearance of James Dallas Egbert III, a student who vanished from Michigan State University in 1979. His full story is sad and complicated. However, the novel, written in a few days' time, claimed that playing RPGs could lead to dissociative and hallucinatory episodes, and suggested that the transition to mature adulthood was found in the voluntary abandonment of the hobby of gaming.

40. A. Preparing to leap off the south tower observation deck of the World Trade Center.

112

Connect the characters from the charming 1980s *Dungeons & Dragons* daytime cartoon show to their role, class, or species.

A. Hank

B. Presto

C. Sheila

D. Eric

E. Uni

F. Diana

G. Bobby

H. Amber

1. Magician

2. Fairie Dragon

3. Acrobat

4. Barbarian

5. Ranger

6. Cavalier

7. Unicorn

8. Thief

41. A. Hank & 5. Ranger. B. Presto & 1. Magician. C. Sheila & 8. Thief. D. Eric & 6. Cavalier. E. Uni & 7. Unicorn. F. Diana & 3. Acrobat. G. Bobby & 4. Barbarian. H. Amber & 2. Fairie Dragon.

6

REALMS

BEYOND

FANTASY

Questions about Other Popular Genres from Sci-Fi Dystopia to Space Adventures to Alternate History Earths

When most people hear "tabletop role-playing game," images of elves and paladins fighting against hordes of orcs pop into their heads. It's that, or images of a bunch of nerds sitting around a table throwing dice and eating chips. Either way, there is no getting around how dominant the fantasy setting has been in the hobby both in terms of games made and space in the public consciousness.

That said, entire worlds exist beyond the regular sword and sorcery for players to explore. Here you will find questions pertaining to games that have more to do with monofilament whips than vorpal blades, and the only fireballs you'll see are coming from the brick of plastique explosives your character smuggled into the megacorporation's bank vault.

While mostly looking at science fiction games, in this chapter, you will also find a few questions about other non-fantasy genres as well: the four-color superheroes of olden times that right wrongs and send crooks to jail; the modern-day schlub that's got a five o'clock shadow, a flask of whiskey, and a clue that needs investigating; the scrounger that just needs to find a fresh source of water so that she can survive one more day in the irradiated desert. All of these and more await the intrepid knowledge seeker that reads on.

Total Possible Points: 58

1

One of the very first science fiction RPGs, *Starfaring* has the classic technobabble reasoning for space travel being easy: crystals. The crystals themselves come in three varieties and are all named after what?

A. Hindu gods

B. Star Trek characters

C. Sci-fi writers

D. Cereal mascots

2

Another one of the earliest sci-fi RPGs, *Traveller*, is still popular to this day. *Traveller* takes a sandbox approach to space adventures with players generally able to make their own fun in the time of the Third Imperium. When exactly *is* the Third Imperium, though?

A. About 360 years in the future

B. About 3,600 years in the future

C. About 36,000 years in the future

D. About 360 years in the past of an alternate timeline

3

The interest of *Traveller* has been such that it has survived and seen almost a dozen different editions since it was originally published in 1977. It has also been adapted into several preexisting systems. Which one of these isn't a version of the game that exists?

A. *GURPS Traveller*, the GURPS system version
B. *Traveller20*, the d20 system version
C. *Traveller HERO*, the hero system version
D. *Traveller the Exploration*, the White Wolf system version

4

The game *Cyberpunk* has had several different versions where the game makers have changed or updated the timeline, so it still takes place far enough in the future. Originally it was *Cyberpunk 2013*, then *Cyberpunk 2020*, and now it is *Cyberpunk RED*. What year does *Cyberpunk RED* take place?

5

True or false?: Hackers in the *Cyberpunk* universe use cybernetic upgrades in order to "jack in" to a virtual world that can look like almost anything. These hackers are known as Cyberdeckers and are fearsome entities in a tech-dependent world.

3. D. *Traveller the Exploration*, the White Wolf system version. 4. 2045. 5. False. They are known as Netrunners and would use cyberdecks as tools.

6

Taking the cyberpunk genre and adding a fantasy twist to it, *Shadowrun* sees players fighting against the megacorps as teched-out Street Samurai, and sometimes the CEO is a dragon. Many humans turned into fantasy races, but there is a specific term for turning into an Orc or a Troll. What is it?

7

Speaking of CEOs being dragons in *Shadowrun*, what is the name of the dragon that owns the megacorporation Saeder-Krupp and is the wealthiest being on the planet?

A. Nachtmeister

B. Feuerschwinge

C. Lofwyr

D. Schwartzkopf

Critical Info

Megacorporations in *Shadowrun* are rated from A to AAA, with most AA and AAA ones being essentially immune to domestic law. Most of them treat the land they own as sovereign territory where the rule of law is entirely their own. Many citizens will have dual citizenship in the nation they are in and the corporation they work for.

6. Goblinized. 7. C. Lofwyr.

8

If there's one thing that any good game set in outer space will have, it's a couple of weird aliens. Maybe they're just humans with weird foreheads. Maybe they are indescribable undulating masses. Match these alien species with the RPG where you can find them.

A. Yazirian

B. Chadra-fan

C. Tellarite

D. Giff

E. Sollemnean

F. Pjanji

G. Zentraedi

H. Ur-Ukar

1. *Star Wars*

2. *Star Frontiers*

3. *The Xro Dinn Chronicles*

4. *Robotech*

5. *Teens in Space*

6. *Fading Suns*

7. *Star Trek*

8. *Spelljammer: Adventures in Space*

8. A. Yazirian & 2. Star Frontiers. B. Chadra-fan & 1. Star Wars. C. Tellarite & 7. Star Trek. D. Giff & 8. Spelljammer: Adventures in Space. E. Sollemnean & 5. Teens in Space. F. Pjanji & 3. The Xro Dinn Chronicles. G. Zentraedi & 4. Robotech. H. Ur-Ukar & 6. Fading Suns.

The big names in sci-fi properties have made many different attempts to translate their beloved settings into RPG books. Which Star Trek game takes place in an entirely alternate history of the classic Star Trek universe?

A. *To Boldly Go*

B. *Prime Directive*

C. *Phaser Blast*

D. *Maximum Overwarp*

Critical Info

The reason that the game takes place in an alternate history of Star Trek isn't the standard reasons of time travel shenanigans or alternate dimensions. Instead, it's because it takes place in the same universe as the Star Fleet Battles wargame, which came out in 1979 and basically had to make up its own expanded universe information and then ignored any of the movies that came after.

10

The current game in the Star Trek universe, *Star Trek Adventures*, allows for players to create and use extra crew members in addition to their main characters in case they want to be in a scene, and it wouldn't make sense for their character to be there. The amount of Crew Support points you get to spend on this is based on what aspect?

11

Star Wars has also had a number of different iterations of their property made into RPGs, though none were quite so influential as *Star Wars: The Roleplaying Game* by West End Games. The sourcebooks for that game would end up establishing much of the expanded universe canon. Which Star Wars alien got their name from the RPG?

A. Twi'lek

B. Rodians

C. Quarren

D. All of the above

12

A more recent RPG set in the Star Wars universe was by Fantasy Flight Games and was released with three different main books to cater to what type of character you wanted to play in the universe. These books were *Star Wars: Edge of the Empire*, *Star Wars: Force and Destiny*, and which other book?

13

Some of the sci-fi properties aren't quite as well-known as others, but that doesn't stop them from getting RPGs. In the game based on the *Red Dwarf* TV series from Britain, players can be Humans, Evolved Pets, Holograms, and even GELFs. What does GELF stand for?

11. D. All of the above. 12. *Star Wars: Age of Rebellion*. 13. Genetically Engineered Life Form.

14

Another beloved British sci-fi show with its own RPG is *Doctor Who*. In the *Doctor Who Roleplaying Game*, violence is not forbidden but is generally discouraged both by the narrative (trying to stop an army of Daleks with a gun is highly unlikely to work) and by the mechanics themselves. What mechanical way does the game accomplish this?

A. Anyone taking a violent action goes last in initiative.
B. Anyone taking a violent action must use a limited resource.
C. Anyone taking a violent action gives the GM a Plot Point to use later.
D. Anyone taking a violent action is immediately scolded by The Doctor.

15

Another game with a focus on dinosaurs and the future is *Cadillacs and Dinosaurs*, based on the comic book series *Xenozoic Tales*. Though the comic series only had fourteen issues and ended mid-story, it spawned a lot of tie-ins in the game. Which of these wasn't a *Cadillacs and Dinosaurs* branded venture?

A. An arcade game
B. A music album

C. A breakfast cereal
D. A cartoon show

14. A. Anyone taking a violent action goes last in initiative. 15. C. A breakfast cereal.

122

16

TSR would try to get in on the space opera RPG action in 1982 with their game *Star Frontiers*. Ironically, it would take almost two years for them to put out a supplement with rules on what?

17

The game *Dinosaur Planet: Broncosaurus Rex* takes place in an alternate version of our future where intelligent space dinosaurs form bonds with their riders. What large historical event changed in our past that caused us to have space dino cowboys?

- **A.** The North lost the American Civil War.
- **B.** Texas seceded from the Union to be its own country.
- **C.** Aliens crashed into California during the Gold Rush.
- **D.** Tesla invented an electric rocket.

Critical Info

Dinosaur Planet: Broncosaurus Rex includes plenty of statistics on the various dinosaurs and their social habits and even, in the case of Tyrannosaurus, psychic abilities. This makes it all the more troublesome when the game talks about using the dinosaurs as beasts of burden, or even food sources, given that they are distinctly sapient.

16. Spaceships. 17. A. The North lost the American Civil War.

123

18

When it comes to sci-fi, *Rifts* has a full kitchen sink policy. It's got space-ships, mechs, lasers, mutants, aliens, and everything in-between. The poster boy for the game and for excessive munitions in general is the Glitter Boy, a mech with a giant and noisy railgun that is colloquially known as what?

19

True or false?: The post-apocalyptic world of *Rifts* Earth includes genetically altered humans that have had their physical abilities drastically increased but with a loss of their mental stability and are known as "Crazies."

20

Not every post-apocalypse gets to have magic and dinosaurs. Some have depressing societal collapse and Cold War–era anxiety settings. *Twilight: 2000* takes place in a world where your characters are survivors of what destructive event?

18. Boom Gun. 19. False. Crazies are a result of nano-tech implants in the brain.
20. World War III.

124

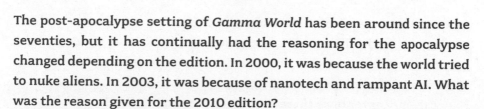

21

The post-apocalypse setting of *Gamma World* has been around since the seventies, but it has continually had the reasoning for the apocalypse changed depending on the edition. In 2000, it was because the world tried to nuke aliens. In 2003, it was because of nanotech and rampant AI. What was the reason given for the 2010 edition?

A. Solar flares irradiated the Earth.
B. The Y2K bug was real and caused nuclear meltdowns.
C. The Large Hadron Collider caused reality to break down.
D. An animal rights group released irradiated animals that conquered the world.

22

In the game *Systems Failure*, the "Millennium Bug" scare of 1999 turned out to be nothing, but then actual giant bugs show up to destroy society instead. In addition to being large and physically powerful, what is it that makes the bugs of *Systems Failure* so uniquely capable of destroying the modern world?

A. They can travel through power/phone lines.
B. They can control computers with their minds.
C. They can lay eggs and spawn on the Internet.
D. They can get you to like and subscribe to their boring vlog.

21. C. The Large Hadron Collider caused reality to break down. 22. A. They can travel through power/phone lines.

23

In the "weird west" of *Deadlands*, there is a mix of horror, western, steampunk, and a little post-apocalypse to keep things spicy. During the game, beings from another dimension are bent on turning Earth into a hellscape via subtle psychic influence and occasional possession, since they can only enter once there is enough of what emotion?

24

True or false?: The steampunk aspects of *Deadlands* come from the discovery of a mineral that burns hotter and longer than coal known as "ghost rock."

25

While generally martial arts-themed, *Feng Shui* also tends to cross into other genres with the inclusion of magic, advanced technology, time travel, and multiple dimensions. With a general feel of an action movie, there are a lot of classes that include you being some kind of cop. Which one of these is not an actual class in *Feng Shui 2*?

A. Karate Cop

B. Magic Cop

C. Maverick Cop

D. Samurai Cop

26

In an ouroboros of theming, *Dream Park: The Roleplaying Game* is based on the book *Dream Park*, which is about an amusement park where people LARP in a holographic game, making this a role-playing game about a book about a role-playing game. What unique aspect of this theme comes into play in the character creation of the game?

A. A player can pick between being a customer, an employee, or a hologram.

B. A player must make two characters: the person they are and their LARP persona.

C. A player can choose a background in LARPing for bonuses to certain rolls.

D. A player must make a character in a different RPG to play in the setting.

27

Set in an alternate version of World War II, *Godlike* is a game that blends the horrors of war with the abilities of superheroes. These empowered people started showing up a few at a time to start, but they appeared more and more as the war went on and could drastically change the outcome. What name does the book use to refer to those with powers?

A. Talents   **B.** Gifted   **C.** Aces   **D.** Demigods

26. B. A player must make two characters: the person they are and their LARP persona.
27. A. Talents.

The game *Unknown Armies* is set in a postmodern version of our world where magic exists, but it takes such a level of belief and obsession to manifest that only the truly unhinged generally manifest it. Match these Adepts with the obsession that gives them their powers.

A. Bibliomancer		**1.** History	
B. Cliomancer		**2.** Alcohol	
C. Dipsomancer		**3.** Sex	
D. Entropomancer		**4.** Risk	
E. Epideromancer		**5.** Subcultures	
F. Plutomancer		**6.** Books	
G. Pornomancer		**7.** Injury	
H. Sociomancer		**8.** Money	

28. A. Bibliomancer & 6. Books. B. Cliomancer & 1. History. C. Dipsomancer & 2. Alcohol. D. Entropomancer & 4. Risk. E. Epideromancer & 7. Injury. F. Plutomancer & 8. Money. G. Pornomancer & 3. Sex. H. Sociomancer & 5. Subcultures.

Critical Info

In addition to Adepts and their obsession-based magic, there are also those that gain supernatural power by adhering to an archetype of humanity so closely that they begin to gain power as an Avatar of it. You don't even need to believe in it. If you act like the Archetype of The Mother hard enough, you get superpowers; that happens even if you actually hate children and taking care of others.

29

True or false?: When aliens learn about teen culture on Earth in the game *Teenagers from Outer Space*, they become so enamored that they let humans attend their schools and players play as either aliens or the humans in the alien school.

30

A bleak look at cyberpunk in the game *SLA Industries* (pronounced "slay") has a future where the titular megacorporation runs not just a large section of the planet but the entire planet and multiple other planets. Players don't generally try to undermine things as much as get by in this dystopian world. The company itself is run by an immortal creature known as what?

A. The Boss   **B.** Overseer   **C.** Mr. Slayer   **D.** Big Sister

29. False. The aliens instead attend Earth schools. 30. C. Mr. Slayer.

31

Like so many sci-fi settings before it, *Eclipse Phase* includes the existence of alien technology that can open wormholes to distant places with no real way to tell where you might end up. The practice of jumping blindly through these Pandora Gates is known as what?

32

True or false?: Divided up into Major and Minor powers, *Heroes Unlimited* has an extensive selection of abilities for would-be superheroes to choose from, including Clock Manipulation, which gives the ability to slow or speed up time.

33

Marvel Comics has had a ton of different RPGs over the years with all sorts of different mechanics and systems in place to help facilitate playing in the Marvel Universe. What mechanic sets *The Marvel Universe Roleplaying Game* (2003) apart from the others?

A. It has no rules for character creation.

B. It is a diceless system.

C. There are no mechanics for combat.

D. There are no rules for being a mutant.

31. Gatecrashing. 32. False. Clock Manipulation just lets you mess with physical clocks. 33. B. It is a diceless system.

True or false?: *There's a Crisis at Crusader Citadel* is an introductory adventure for *Villains and Vigilantes* that has players controlling neophyte heroes that should be based on the players themselves.

The *Marvel Super Heroes* RPG, first published in 1984, uses a system often referred to as FASERIP due to the stats in the game having that as an acronym. All of the stats and powers in the game, instead of being represented solely by a number, are also represented by a name. So, for example, you wouldn't have a Flight Score of 100, you would have Unearthly Flight. Put these descriptors in order from most to least powerful.

A. Incredible

B. Excellent

C. Good

D. Amazing

E. Remarkable

F. Monstrous

G. Shift X

H. Poor

Critical Info

The list for descriptors tends to pull from some of the Marvel properties, such as "Incredible" from the Hulk or "Amazing" from Spider-Man. Strangely, they used some generic terms, while there are still some clearly absent choices, such as "Uncanny" (X-Men), "Fantastic" (Four), "Spectacular" (Spider-Man), or "Mighty" (Thor).

34. True. 35. From Most to Least Powerful: G. Shift X, F. Monstrous, D. Amazing, A. Incredible, E. Remarkable, B. Excellent, C. Good, H. Poor.

36

True or false?: The West End Games Star Wars material was considered to be so authoritative that when Timothy Zahn was hired to write the Thrawn trilogy of books, Lucasfilm sent him a box of RPG books to use as background material.

37

The Mayfair Games' *DC Heroes* RPG had a number of character attributes to represent Strength or Dexterity like most other games. What made the attributes unique is in the way the game would scale them for heroes such that you could have Batman and Superman reflected in the same stats. How did they accomplish this?

- **A.** Attributes have a parenthetical number in addition to a base number that you multiply it by.
- **B.** Attributes would scale on a multiple of 10s with Superman having a Strength in the thousands.
- **C.** Attributes would scale logarithmically so 3 is twice as powerful as 2, 4 twice as powerful as 3, and so on.
- **D.** The attributes didn't have numbers but descriptive names such as Human, Amazon, or Kryptonian for strength.

36. True. 37. C. Attributes would scale logarithmically so 3 is twice as powerful as 2, 4 twice as powerful as 3, and so on.

38

One of the earliest superhero games was *Champions*, and it was also one of the first to use a point-buy system for its character generation. The rules for the game were popular enough that they were adapted into a generic game system appropriately titled what?

39

Focused on teen heroes, *Masks: A New Generation* has a number of playbooks that focus more on what type of hero you are in personality and how you approach being a hero than on your powerset. What playbook named after a Roman deity is all about the dichotomy of superhero and secret identity?

40

True or false?: The latest Marvel RPG to be released at this time, *Marvel Multiverse Role-Playing Game*, uses the d616 system, named after the main Marvel universe being designated 616 in-universe.

7

JEWEL-LIKE OBJECTS OF WONDER

Questions about Minis and the Games That Use Them, Like *Warhammer*, Gundam-Driven Games, and Other Classic Wargames

If you were to trace *D&D* far enough back along its evolutionary history, you'd eventually reach a point where Gary Gygax's *Chainmail* turns up (actually, it'll turn up a few times along the way, but that's branding for you!). *Chainmail* is a game of moving squads and battalions of tiny warriors, as well as powerful monsters and war machines. Yes, *D&D* is born of wargame roots, with the original game being mass battles between soldiers, wizards, balrogs (the monster from The Lord of the Rings series indeed; early wargame history wasn't quite as concerned with trademarks as we are nowadays), and ranked mass cavalry.

Gygax was a wargamer before he and Dave Arneson ever thought to focus on the individual stories of a few of the heroes of their massive tabletop battles. Before and since then, wargames have enjoyed a great deal of popularity as another way to enact all the geeky stories we love to tell. Today, there are dozens of wargames commonly played in game stores and conventions across the world, complete with their own industry-dominating juggernauts (hello *Warhammer!*). Of course, as with RPGs, there are myriad challengers to that dominance introducing their particular flavor of cool or more realistic rules, ever more intricate miniatures, and heaps upon heaps of dice to roll.

1

With the somewhat unwieldy title of *Little Wars: a game for boys from twelve years of age to one hundred and fifty and for that more intelligent sort of girl who likes boys' games and books*, *Little Wars* (for short) is a well-known older rule book for miniature combat, having been written in 1913. Which famous novelist from the era wrote it?

A. Edgar Rice Burroughs

B. H.G. Wells

C. Sigmund Freud

D. W.B. Yeats

Critical Info

Some of the earliest known mass-produced miniatures used for play were manufactured in Germany in the 1700s out of tin. They were literally called *Zinnfiguren*, or "tin soldiers." Over the centuries, a variety of materials have been used including various metals, plastics, and even compressed paper. During the era of early RPG design, lead was popular for its malleability, weight, and cost. Unfortunately, it's not especially safe to handle and was banned across the US during the early 1990s, with industry juggernaut Games Workshop finally abandoning all lead in miniatures in 1997.

1. B. H.G. Wells.

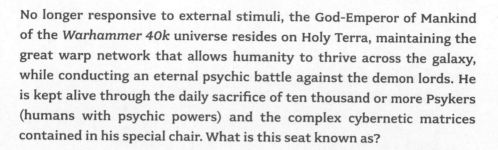

2

No longer responsive to external stimuli, the God-Emperor of Mankind of the *Warhammer 40k* universe resides on Holy Terra, maintaining the great warp network that allows humanity to thrive across the galaxy, while conducting an eternal psychic battle against the demon lords. He is kept alive through the daily sacrifice of ten thousand or more Psykers (humans with psychic powers) and the complex cybernetic matrices contained in his special chair. What is this seat known as?

3

What medieval wargame, written in 1967 by Henry Bodenstedt, would *D&D* creator Gary Gygax play at the first GenCon in 1968, inspiring him and Jeff Perrin to eventually create their own wargame, *Chainmail*?

A. *Siege of Bodenburg*
B. *Quacks of Quedlinburg*

C. *The Sacking of Monschau*
D. *Dardanelles: 1915*

4

Draw a line connecting these cool tabletop hero miniatures to the game they come from. Note that some or maybe even all of these characters are technically represented in a number of tabletop games (there are just *so many* miniature wargames), we've just carefully ensured that only one game matches in the list.

A. **Captain Gunnbjorn**

B. **Lograx**

C. **Lucius Gustavius FitzWilliam Mattheson**

D. **Kenaz Stoneheart**

E. **Van Zant**

F. **Aurora, Numen of Aerogenesis**

G. **Avarisse & Greede**

H. **Gor Half-Horn**

1. *Infinity*

2. *Malifaux*

3. *Guild Ball*

4. *Necromunda*

5. *Warmachine*

6. *Star Wars: Shatterpoint*

7. *Hordes*

8. *Mage Knight*

5

Of the various units of Orks that make up the grand WAAAGHs of *Warhammer 40k* space, which group of boys are obsessed with their customized, carefully polished, and almost well-maintained giant guns, which they refer to as "snazzguns"?

6

True or false?: Recently returned to the *Warhammer 40k* army list with a brand-new roster and an extraordinary glow up on their model range, the Leagues of Votann faction is an update on the classic army of "Abhuman" dwarf figures known colloquially as the Squats. The first time they were removed from the range of figures, it was explained in-universe as an incident in which their home world was devoured by a Tyranid Hive Fleet.

7

True or false?: According to *D&D* cocreator Dave Arneson, the Cleric class in *D&D* was originally introduced in his Chainmail miniatures *Blackmoor* game as a direct opposite to a specific vampire played by one of the players, named Sir Fang.

8

The Cicatrix Maledictum is a chain of terrifying warp rifts disgorging destruction and foul demons of the warp, while dividing the galaxy nearly in two. It was created at the end of the forty-first millennium immediately following the destruction of Cadia during the thirteenth Black Crusade (*Warhammer 40k* is nothing if not metal). The destruction broke up ancient trade routes and alliances over uncountably vast distances. What is this chain of events more commonly known as?

A. The Sundering

B. The Hellstorm Line

C. The Great Rift

D. The Crimson Highway

9

The fearsome Vampire Counts faction of *Warhammer Fantasy* set out from the lands of Sylvania to attempt to conquer the Empire itself. This faction is composed of the heads of various noble vampire families, their powerful thralls and necromantic creations, and various twisted ghosts and horrors that prowl the night. Who is the leader of this dark army?

A. Count Warlock

B. Settra the Imperishable

C. Count Vlad von Carstein

D. Dracula Unrolled

When a *Warhammer 40k* Space Marine's already formidable immense size, regular suit of plasteel and adamantine power armor, holy bolter rocket rifle, intensive genetic modifications, and incredible training aren't enough to get the job done, they may use suits of powerful battle armor with thick plating and teleportation capacity. This armor is formerly known as Tactical Dreadnought Armour, but what's the informal name for it and the marines that utilize it?

A. MK III Iron Armour

B. Terminator Armour

C. Dreadknight

D. Imperius Plate

Critical Info

Primarch (the genetic "father") of the Ultramarines Roboute Guilliman may have died in the 30Ks, but he was resurrected and contributed to the Space Marine workforce ten thousand years later. He later introduced the concept of Primaris Space Marines, a new breed of bigger, stronger, and more capable marines than the already incredibly powerful marines of the Legiones Astartes. (His invention luckily coincided with Games Workshop's need to sell new Space Marine models along with the release of the 8th edition of their *Warhammer 40K* rule set in 2017!) In the lore, Primaris Space Marines can be bred new, or existing marines can undergo a dangerous and painful procedure called the Rubicon Primaris to become one.

11

The T'au are an impressively powerful race within the galaxy of *Warhammer 40k*. They are masters of combined arms and battlefield tactics and will ally with other races to utilize each species' unique strengths in wartime instead of just obliterating all they come across. The T'au Empire (their area of space, marked by growth periods known as Spheres of Expansion) grows daily thanks to their relatively harmonious caste-based governing system. Which T'au commander has been called a renegade by his own race?

A. O'Shovah, Commander Farsight
B. Aun'Shi, Hero of Fio'vash
C. Shaserra, Commander Shadowsun
D. O'O'O'O'Reilly, Autarch Parts

12

True or false?: Asmodee, a French games distributor, currently produces *X-Wing*, a tabletop ship combat game that features *Star Wars* heroes piloting the many signature ships of that universe. One of the original ships from that line is the Imperial Unit the Alpha-Class XG-1 Star Wing.

11. A. O'Shovah, Commander Farsight. 12. False. This relatively unknown ship first appeared in the MS-DOS and PC game *Star Wars: X-Wing*, published in 1993 by LucasArts.

142

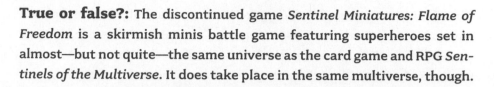

13

True or false?: The discontinued game *Sentinel Miniatures: Flame of Freedom* is a skirmish minis battle game featuring superheroes set in almost—but not quite—the same universe as the card game and RPG *Sentinels of the Multiverse*. It does take place in the same multiverse, though.

14

The High Elves of *Warhammer Fantasy* are led by two primary monarchs, the Phoenix King and his chosen ritual consort, the Everqueen. As Everqueens enjoy a lifelong position after their appointment, it is not uncommon for them to outlive multiple Phoenix Kings, and they are further unbound by the legal requirements of office that the King must abide by. They instead answer to the callings of Isha, the High Elven goddess of nature and fertility. Who currently reigns as the High Elven Everqueen?

A. Alarielle the Radiant

B. Estrielle the Silver

C. Yvraine the Chaotic

D. Fenthyra the Damp

15

What living metal vehicle/building do Necrons (a race of metallic skeleton warriors in the *Warhammer 40k* universe) use to arrive instantaneously onto battlefields? (These vehicle/buildings allow the Necron soldiers to march to the battle directly through warp gates located on its sides.)

Critical Info

If you ever find yourself at a game convention and hear a *WAAAAAGH* sound coming from the wargame tables, don't worry, it's just *Warhammer 40k* Ork players expressing themselves. This term is a generic catch-all expression of victory, intent to achieve victory, intent to claim revenge, and the term to describe the act of making war in any large, noteworthy capacity. It's caught on among the fanbase, and even players of more sedate, less bloodthirsty armies (just kidding, they're all pretty bloodthirsty) will join in a good *WAAAGH* when they hear one. Give it a try, it's cathartic!

16

True or false?: The WizKids games *Star Trek: Attack Wing* and *Dungeons & Dragons: Attack Wing* are based on the same rules as the Asmodee game *Star Wars: X-Wing*.

Connect the names of each Tyranid Biomorph (a fearsome, extra-galactic invader) with the Latin or Greek meaning of their Empire-assigned designation. You may notice the two primary sub-themes of Tyranid naming, which are Roman military ranks and five-dollar words that boil down to variations of "mean lady" because in the far future, people are bad at naming cool bugs.

A. Exocrine

B. Termagant

C. Carnifex

D. Gargoyle

E. Haruspex

F. Zoanthrope

G. Dimachaeron

H. Heirodule

1. Temple Prostitute

2. Gargling Sound

3. Unpleasant Older Woman

4. Bearing Two Knives

5. Executioner of a Roman Army

6. External Secretion

7. The Belief That One Is an Animal

8. Priest or Diviner

17. A. Exocrine & 6. External Secretion. B. Termagant & 3. Unpleasant Older Woman. C. Carnifex & 5. Executioner of a Roman Army. D. Gargoyle & 2. Gargling Sound. E. Haruspex & 8. Priest or Diviner. F. Zoanthrope & 7. The Belief That One Is an Animal. G. Dimarchaeron & 4. Dealling Two Knives. H. Heirodule & 1. Temple Prostitute.

The Wyrd world of the game *Malifaux* is set in the 1900s. The original Earth of this setting is twisted and bizarre, an alternate history in which steampunk and magic reign supreme, largely as a result of the discovery of a permanent portal to a horrifying and unreal alternate dimension known as *Malifaux* where powerful resources await those canny enough to claim them. What is the name of the original inhabitants of the *Malifaux* world?

A. The Twisted

B. Neverborn

C. Mirror Mortals

D. Reflects

19

Which Dwarf faction in *Warhammer Age of Sigmar* utilizes steampunk metal blimps and flying armor suits to take to the skies in pursuit of their enemies?

18. B. Neverborn. 19. Kharadron Overlords.

20

Many factions in the *Warmachine* setting make use of Warcasters (arcane people who form bonds with their semi-autonomous bipedal war machines: either steamjacks or warjacks). This has led to the destruction of the machines and war with other factional heroes and villains. One faction, however, chooses to take direct control of their war creations, eschewing any semblance of semi-sentience and, instead, controlling every move their machines, known as "Vectors," make. Which faction is this?

A. Convergence of Cyriss   **C.** The Talion Charter
B. Cryx   **D.** The Silver Banshees

21

Which of the following Marvel comics characters in the game *Marvel: Crisis Protocol* (a Marvel-themed tabletop miniature game) is modeled astride a massive, winged tiger?

A. Malekith   **B.** Gwenpool   **C.** MODOK   **D.** Tigerella

22

Chainmail experienced a brief resurgence as a WOTC-produced miniature skirmish game in 2000, launching alongside a series of miniatures divided up into factions that represented Dwarves, Humans, Elves, Gnolls, and more. The character units used simplified versions of D&D stat blocks to participate in battles to claim ground and defeat the enemy units. What was the name of the Drow faction in WOTC *Chainmail*?

A. Ravila

B. Drazen's Horde

C. Drow Boyz

D. Kilsek

Critical Info

With the sheer amount of careful sculpting and design that goes into modern minis, you might think collectors would build and paint them exactly as the manufacturer intended. However, many nerds want to tinker, and the practice of "kitbashing" is one of the most celebrated parts of the hobby! Adding parts from different models to create a custom piece is one way to go, but many modelers sculpt additions to minis themselves, thanks to epoxy putties such as Kneadatite. These putties, originally developed for automotive repair, have exactly the right set of properties for holding shape, curing quickly, and accepting paints to allow art-minded hobbyists to make their own alterations.

22. D. Kilsek.

23

True or false?: Aspect Warriors are specialized units of Eldar that focus on perfection in specific battlefield roles. Of these aspects, the Fire Dragons are specialists in cracking armored vehicles and similarly tough targets.

24

What game, published by Warcradle Studios and released in 2011, features battles between super-science-equipped warships on, above, and below the ocean, taking place in an alternate history during the 1870s?

25

True or false?: The Tyranid Biomorphs bred exclusively to shield and defend the powerful and psychically dominating Hive Tyrants are called the Biovore.

23. True. 24. *Dystopian Wars.* 25. False. Biovores are living artillery units that launch projectiles over vast distances. The bioform tasked with defending Hive Tyrants is the heavily armored Hive Guard.

149

26

In 2005, Mongoose Publishing released *Starship Troopers: The Miniatures Game*, a skirmish tabletop battle game focused on characters from the film and book of the same name. It was immensely popular for a brief period, but it quickly dried up and vanished by 2008. In addition to the humans and famous bugs of the film, what third faction was added to the game, taken directly from the original Robert A. Heinlein novel?

A. Zombies   **B.** Skinnies   **C.** Capitalism   **D.** The Greys

27

HeroClix is a line of collectible miniatures produced by The Topps Company that have been around since 2002. Models sit on custom bases with rotating dials that allow information about the character to change over the course of a combat. While focused on DC or Marvel comic book heroes, the company has held licenses to produce models from many other intellectual properties (Ips) over the years. Which of the following IPs has not been utilized by HeroClix?

A. Assassin's Creed   **C.** Iron Maiden
B. Yu-Gi-Oh!   **D.** KISS

28

True or false?: The variant of *Warhammer 40k* that arrays vast armies (up to entire houses of knightly orders and chapters of marines) and allows the fielding of mighty Forge World Titans and other massive models is called "Ragnarök."

29

Which faction in the Privateer Press game *Hordes* is composed primarily of human druids, werewolves, and sentient stone constructs?

30

Knight Models began publishing the *Batman Miniature Game* in 2012, and since then it has allowed players to battle it out on the streets of Gotham. The game pits the many costumed villains' gangs against each other, as well as against the Dark Knight and his allies. Who is the obscure, playable villain in this system that wears an old-fashioned camera on his head like a helmet?

A. The Photographer

B. Mr. Camera

C. Snapshot

D. The Riddler's Weird Nephew

28. False. This massive cinematic mode of play that can take entire days and fill up game stores is actually known as Apocalypse. 29. The Circle Orboros. 30. B. Mr. Camera.

31

In *Warmachine*, under what charter of piracy does the warcaster for the Mercarian League, Captain Phinneus Shae, and his mighty deck gun, the Commodore Cannon, sail?

32

True or false?: Between 2004 and 2008, a game called *Pirates: The Constructible Strategy Game* was produced by Wizards of the Coast. This collectible card game had packs that came with two punch-out plastic cards that could be assembled into pirate ships. It also included rare sea monsters such as an enormous crab.

33

Which of the following teams is *not* a canon squad from the Games Workshop game *Blood Bowl*, in which teams of fantasy warriors and monsters take to the pitch to play a slightly silly but very brutal and dangerous game of football?

A. The Stunted Stoutfellows

C. The Greenskins Pigskin

B. Dwarf Giants

D. Lowdown Rats

31. The Talion Charter. 32. True. 33. C. The Greenskins Pigskin.

152

34

Historical World War II miniature combat game *Flames of War* will often include real veterans of the war as playable miniatures to honor their service and grant them special abilities on the battlefield. In cases where the game's makers wish to honor groups of people or special events or equipment, they will create fictional "warriors" meant to evoke those influences. Which *Flames of War* warrior represents the importance of the 6-Pounder (the British 57-millimeter anti-tank gun) during the D-Day invasion of Normandy?

- **A.** Tom Stanley
- **B.** Dick Bong
- **C.** Richard Ball
- **D.** Lord Wembley Chesterstroke

35

What company produces the miniature skirmish game *Infinity*, in which small teams of futuristic cyberpunk-inspired high-tech warriors engage in fierce gun battles with robots, aliens, and anime-themed battlers?

34. A. Tom Stanley. 35. Corvus Belli.

True or false?: The miniature skirmish game *Kombat: Rise of the Lin-Kuei* is based on the adventures of the various murderous martial artists of the *Mortal Kombat* universe, and features fatalities and brutalities, as well as friendships, provided you have purchased the corresponding expansions.

Critical Info

Though there are a few games (*HeroClix*, *X-Wing*, etc.) that require little or no hobby tools or skills beyond knowledge of gameplay, most miniature wargames are a series of linked hobbies. Between kitbashing to create the perfect figure, painting, basing, and coming up with safe storage and transport solutions, it's amazing that anyone has time to play these games! Plus, there's competitions and accolades available at any level of hobby participation, with the Golden Demon awards for excellent painting and miniature conversion being ranked as highly as actual tournament awards in the minds of many players.

36. False. This is just untrue. Our writers made this one up.

Draw a line connecting each of these *Warhammer 40k* Chapter Masters (the illustrious Firstborn or Primaris Space Marines that serve as the lords and commanding officers) with their respective Chapters of Space Marines.

A. High Marshal Helbrecht

B. Dante

C. Kaldor Draigo

D. Asterion Moloc

E. Jubal Khan

F. Marneus Augustus Calgar

G. Gabriel Angelos

H. Tu'Shan

1. Blood Ravens

2. Black Templars

3. White Scars

4. Blood Angels

5. Ultramarines

6. Grey Knights

7. Salamanders

8. Minotaurs

37. A. High Marshal Helbrecht & 2. Black Templars. B. Dante & 4. Blood Angels. C. Kaldor Draigo & 6. Grey Knights. D. Asterion Moloc & 8. Minotaurs. E. Jubal Khan & 3. White Scars. F. Marneus Augustus Calgar & 5. Ultramarines. G. Gabriel Angelos & 1. Blood Ravens. H. Tu'Shan & 7. Salamanders.

38

In the Warhammer Fantasy universe, what name is given to the most honored of Dwarven warriors, whose facial hair is lengthy enough to touch the ground?

39

Which of the four ruinous major powers of Chaos in the Warhammer and 40K universes represents excess, sensation, depravity, grace, and indulgence?

40

What game, originally introduced by Games Workshop in 1999, was a version of their Warhammer Fantasy line intended to model combats at smaller skirmish scales?

38. Longbeards. 39. Slaanesh. 40. Mordheim.

True or false?: There are two things known as the Carnifex in *Warhammer 40k*, the enormously destructive Tyranid monster (sometimes referred to as the Screamer-Killer) and the upgraded machine gun variation of the Space Marine's trusty bolter rifle.

41. False. The Space Marine Carnifex is not a machine gun, but rather a tool held by the support apothecaries of the marines. It's used to quickly and painlessly kill marines too wounded to continue fighting.

MODERN-DAY CLASSICS

Questions about Recent Entries in the Evolution of Gaming

The role-playing game has had a history of constant evolution and change. Writers get inspired by a game that they have played and want to create something new with their own vision. Since the mid-2000s, RPGs have had a renaissance with players and creators alike delving into what makes a game worthwhile both in terms of the mechanics and the role-playing.

This chapter looks at the games and trends that have dominated the RPG space over the last few years. There are games and designers that have become popular enough to rival the great D&D for recognizability and shelf space in local stores. These range from mainstream names that any gamer would know to some indie darlings that managed to make a big splash on the scene.

The questions in this chapter vary widely and are about all kinds of genres and rule sets. There are games represented with lighter rule sets that focus on character above all else, but there are also games that want to hearken back to the feel of gaming from yesteryear. The only thread that ties these games together is that they all draw from the rich history of role-playing to create a new and modern take. These games provide a platform where people can get lost in their love for the hobby, and they may perhaps inspire the next generation of game designers.

Total Possible Points: 58

1

Many of the more famous modern-day designers were able to workshop their ideas and discuss design on an infamous Internet forum in the early 2000s. It would spawn all sorts of theories on game design that are still used today. What was the name of that forum?

A. The Guild

B. The Forge

C. The Imaginarium

D. Something Awful

2

One of the most influential modern-day games comes from Meguey and David Vincent Baker in a post-apocalyptic setting. The rules were made open to use and became extremely popular for modern designers. What is the name of that original game?

3

True or false?: The original playbooks for the Baker's apocalyptic setting all came with "Sex Moves" that could only be activated if the character got down and dirty.

1. B. The Forge. 2. Apocalypse World 3. True.

4

Powered by the Apocalypse (PbtA) is such a widespread rule system that it has been adapted into all sorts of settings and games that aren't anything like the original. What is the name of the game that takes those rules and attempts to make a game that emulates *Dungeons & Dragons*?

5

Using the PbtA system and inspired by shows like *Buffy the Vampire Slayer*, *X-Files*, *Supernatural*, and *Power Rangers*, this game gained more fame when it was used in season 2 of the *Adventure Zone* podcast. What is the name of the game?

6

True or false?: The superhero PbtA game *Masks: A New Generation* is based on superheroes that take over when all the old ones disappear suddenly.

4. *Dungeon World*. 5. *Monster of the Week*. 6. False. The game is about young teen heroes in the manner of *Teen Titans*.

161

7

A generic game like the classic *GURPS*, *FATE* set its design apart by having a more modern focus on character aspects than crunchy rules and statistics. The popular game itself was mostly based on what preexisting system?

A. Role Free

C. Unbound Worlds

B. Drama System

D. Fudge

8

Pathfinder is a game that has set itself up as a direct alternative to *Dungeons & Dragons* with some decent success. It was actually born out of a decision that *D&D* made. What was the reason for its creation?

A. The abandoning of Vancian casting

B. The loss of signature characters

C. The move from 3.5 to 4th edition

D. A dare from Gary Gygax

7. D. Fudge. 8. C. The move from 3.5 to 4th edition.

9

True or false?: *Pathfinder* made a hardline stance that certain species are always evil, such as the Dark Elves, but they have changed their ruling on this in recent years.

10

In the second edition of *Pathfinder*, the core rulebook was reworked to balance around a more cohesive structure. One of the things that got reworked was Paladin just being the lawful good version of what new core class?

Critical Info

The new version of a Paladin-like class is less restrictive because it allows a player to be something other than lawful good. However, the core class is still restricted to any of the good alignments. Though supplements have come out to allow those players fixated on evil variants to make their Antipaladins.

11

Some modern games have tried to branch out to make mechanics fit the themes of their games by getting the players to engage with the game in a new way. One horror game accomplished this by using a Jenga tower instead of dice. What is the name of that game?

12

Using the mechanic of a Jenga tower is also the main way players interact in the game *Star Crossed*. The players are two people that are attracted to each other but can't (or shouldn't) act on that urge. What happens when/ if the tower should fall?

A. The characters part, never to meet again
B. The characters give in to their temptation
C. The characters' love turns to hate
D. The characters die

13

True or false?: With a variety of different genres but a focus on investigative work, the GUMSHOE system has players roll handfuls of dice to figure out clues.

11. *Dread.* 12. B. The characters give in to their temptation. 13. False. The system rolls 1 die with points spent to increase the roll.

14

Played mostly as an improv storytelling game that bills itself as being able to make your own Coen Brothers movie, what game uses two colors of dice only as a means of generating ideas rather than resolution?

A. *The Failures*

B. *Downward Spiral*

C. *Catastrophe*

D. *Fiasco*

15

One popular Gumshoe game features the players as government agents dealing with vampiric problems, including an entire supplement dedicated to that old rascal Dracula. What is the name of this game?

A. *Night's Black Agents*

B. *Night's Holy Liaison*

C. *New Fang Lords*

D. *Midnight League Bastion*

Critical Info

The supplement all about Dracula is called *The Dracula Dossier* and is about one thousand pages long and spans three different books. One of them is set up as the full text of the original Dracula novel with certain changes and notes throughout from in-universe characters that were looking into the real Dracula.

14. D. *Fiasco*. 15. A. *Night's Black Agents*.

16

One of the most influential games recently has been *Blades in the Dark*. There has been a whole collection of different settings to run the system in, but the base setting is a mix of Victorian England with urban fantasy elements. In this city, the sun no longer shines. What is the city's name?

A. Fallenel   **B.** Doskvol   **C.** Darrini   **D.** Ungland

True or false?: The system for *Blades in the Dark*, Forged in the Dark, has become a popular one for people to create games in since it only takes a small fee to license the system.

True or false?: The *Blades in the Dark* system has been adapted to some genres that are pretty far from the thieves and smugglers of the original game. This includes *Girl by Moonlight*, a *Sailor Moon*–inspired setting.

16. B. Doskvol. 17. False. It is freely usable under the Creative Commons License. 18. True.

19

The 2000s saw a boom in the ability of TV shows, books, and movies to all have their own RPG. Match up the media property with the game system it was based in.

A. *Buffy the Vampire Slayer*

B. *Discworld*

C. *Firefly*

D. *Stargate: SG-1*

E. *Doctor Who*

F. *Star Wars*
(Fantasy Flight Games edition)

G. *Avatar: The Last Airbender*

H. *Conan*

1. GURPS Lite

2. Cortex Action

3. Vortex

4. Unisystem

5. 2d20 System

6. Narrative Dice System

7. d20 System

8. Powered by the Apocalypse

19. A. *Buffy the Vampire Slayer* & 4. Unisystem. B. *Discworld* & 1. GURPS Lite. C. *Firefly* & 2. Cortex Action. D. *Stargate: SG-1* & 7. d20 System. E. *Doctor Who* & 3. Vortex. F. *Star Wars* (Fantasy Flight Games edition) & 6. Narrative Dice System. G. *Avatar: The Last Airbender* & 8. Powered by the Apocalypse. H. *Conan* & 5. 2d20 System.

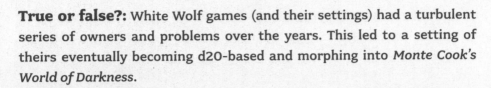

20

True or false?: White Wolf games (and their settings) had a turbulent series of owners and problems over the years. This led to a setting of theirs eventually becoming d20-based and morphing into *Monte Cook's World of Darkness*.

Critical Info

In 2006, White Wolf got purchased by CCP Games, the company that makes *EVE Online*, when CCP Games thought they were going to make games based in the setting. They didn't and this led to them being purchased by Paradox Interactive, another video game company, which got into immediate trouble for referencing neo-Nazis and real-world atrocities. So, yeah, not the best track record for video game companies and White Wolf.

21

True or false?: With the ability to play as Unicorns, Pegasi, Earth ponies, or Alicorns (a blend of all three), the *My Little Pony: Tails of Equestria* RPG is an easy way to get kids into the hobby.

20. True. 21. False. You cannot play as an Alicorn.

168

22

The Burning Wheel came out in 2002 and had the standard Tolkien fantasy trappings of Men, Elves, Dwarves, and Orcs. The non-humans are generally more powerful than their counterparts, but they suffer from an attribute that can make them unplayable if pushed too far. Dwarves have Greed. Orcs have Hatred. What do Elves have?

A. Whimsy   **B.** Ennui   **C.** Fatalism   **D.** Grief

23

While it has had several revisions, the latest addition to The Burning Wheel games is a setting based on a comic book about adorable anthropomorphic creatures in a pseudo-medieval setting. What is the name of that comic/game?

24

True or false?: *Eclipse Phase* is an RPG set after a World War III artificial intelligence project known as TITAN created world peace and helped humankind explore the stars.

22. D. Grief. 23. *Mouse Guard* 24. False. TITAN wiped out over 90 percent of humanity and humans abandoned Earth.

169

25

Plenty of games are based on standard narrative media, as evidenced by plenty of the questions in this book. Not many are based solely on art, however. What is the alternate history science fiction RPG that is based on the art of Simon Stålenhag?

A. *The Electric State*

B. *Tales from the Loop*

C. *Ripple in Time*

D. *Verge of the Future*

26

The game *Kids on Bikes* is inspired by classic 1980s coming-of-age movies like *The Goonies*, and it's great for people that want a game with a vibe similar to *Stranger Things*. It has options for "powered" characters, like E.T. or Eleven, that can join the kids, but what restraint is put on them?

A. The other players can exert narrative control on them.

B. They pass out if they use their powers too much.

C. They are doomed to leave after a certain amount of time.

D. They can only have bike-related powers.

25. B. *Tales from the Loop.* 26. A. The other players can exert narrative control on them.

170

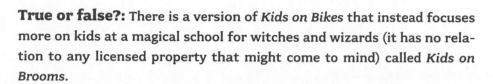

27

True or false?: There is a version of *Kids on Bikes* that instead focuses more on kids at a magical school for witches and wizards (it has no relation to any licensed property that might come to mind) called *Kids on Brooms*.

28

The modern RPG landscape is filled with acronyms like *D&D* instead of *Dungeons & Dragons* or *PbtA* in place of *Powered by the Apocalypse*. What does the acronym *DCC* stand for?

A. *Dungeons, Critters, and Casters*
B. *Dungeon Crawl Classics*
C. *Draconic Creature Class*
D. *Deadly Critical Clash*

29

Some old games have had new life breathed into them by being brought into a new system. What classic RPG was revitalized in the Savage Worlds system?

A. *Tunnels & Trolls*   **C.** *TORG*
B. *Pendragon*   **D.** *Rifts*

30

The ENNIES are one of the few prestigious awards that RPGs can get. Match up these award-winning RPGs with the category that they took gold in.

A. *Eclipse Phase*

B. *ALIEN: The Roleplaying Game*

C. *Continuity*

D. *No Thank You, Evil!*

E. *Cthulhu by Gaslight*

F. *Heart: The City Beneath*

G. *Delta Green*

H. *NPC Codex*

1. Best Supplement

2. Best Game

3. Product of the Year

4. Best Writing

5. Best Layout and Design

6. Best Electronic Book

7. Best Family Game

8. Best Rules

30. A. *Eclipse Phase* & 4. Best Writing. B. *ALIEN: The Roleplaying Game* & 2. Best Game. C. *Continuity* & 6. Best Electronic Book. D. *No Thank You, Evil!* & 7. Best Family Game. E. *Cthulhu by Gaslight* & 1. Best Supplement. F. *Heart: The City Beneath* & 5. Best Layout and Design. G. *Delta Green* & 8. Best Rules. H. *NPC Codex* & 3. Product of the Year.

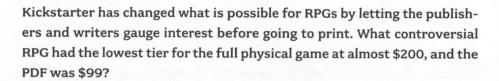

31

Kickstarter has changed what is possible for RPGs by letting the publishers and writers gauge interest before going to print. What controversial RPG had the lowest tier for the full physical game at almost $200, and the PDF was $99?

A. *The World's Largest Dungeon*   **C.** *Invisible Sun*
B. *Compleat Traveller*   **D.** *Actual Gold*

Critical Info

The Kickstarter for the physical product also came with an entire box full of weird little trinkets and doodads, including a large plastic hand that would hold one of the cards from the deck that the game came with. It provided no other function or purpose, but you could purchase additional hands for $23 each.

32

When it comes to talking about record-breaking RPGs on Kickstarter, it would be impossible not to mention the game that made more money than any other. What game based on a kids' TV show has, at the time of this writing, the highest-grossing Kickstarter for an RPG?

31. C. *Invisible Sun.* 32. *Avatar Legends: The Roleplaying Game.*

33

An entire genre of microgames came to the forefront in the modern design space recently; these games could fit entirely on a single sheet of paper, and some contained no more than two hundred words. What influential microgame is a pastiche of *Star Trek* with only two stats you can roll?

34

Writer Grant Howitt has become well established for his microgames that span different genres and are able to hit their mark with limited space. What is the name of his microgame about bears trying to steal honey?

A. *Honey Heist*
B. *Bearly Capable*
C. *Furry Filchers*
D. *The Woodland Job*

35

Even in the modern day, people still want to take *D&D* and improve upon it. What game written by two previous *D&D* head writers gave characters more free-form backgrounds and each *One Unique Thing* in their creation?

36

It would be impossible to talk about modern RPGs without at least acknowledging the major impact that 5th edition *D&D* has had on the hobby. Which of the following actual-play shows is the only one to not use 5E *D&D*?

A. *Critical Role*

B. *Dimension 20*

C. *Dungeons & Daddies*

D. *Party of One*

Most classes and races are fairly consistent between editions, but 4th edition *D&D* added two new core classes. Of those, only the Warlock managed to become a core class in the 5th edition. What amazing class didn't manage to find its way into the next edition?

Critical Info

The Warlock was originally introduced midway through 3.5E *D&D* as a non-core class in the *Complete Arcane* book. It was the first caster that didn't actually cast spells and didn't have the same spell slot limitation of other casters. The "at will" use of abilities presaged the At Will powers of the 4th edition.

36. D. Party of One. 37. The Warlord.

38

If there's one thing the modern-day creators of Dungeons & Dragons recognize, it's the inherent desire of players to make animal people. Whether you're a furry or just like the idea of getting in touch with your wild side, there have never been more animal options. Match these D&D race options with the animal that they are based on.

A. Aarakocra

B. Giff

C. Hadozee

D. Harengon

E. Kenku

F. Leonin

G. Loxodon

H. Tabaxi

1. Rabbit

2. Elephant

3. Cat

4. Lion

5. Eagle

6. Monkey

7. Raven

8. Hippopotamus

38. A. Aarakocra & 5. Eagle. B. Giff & 8. Hippopotamus. C. Hadozee & 6. Monkey. D. Harengon & 1. Rabbit. E. Kenku & 7. Raven. F. Leonin & 4. Lion. G. Loxodon & 2. Elephant. H. Tabaxi & 3. Cat.

39

An indie game by *Apocalypse World* creators David Vincent Baker called *Dogs in the Vineyard* won multiple awards when it came out, but it is no longer available due to his dissatisfaction with the setting. What is the setting for the game?

A. You play as enforcers in a fictional version of the West.
B. You play as dogs protecting a farm in the post-apocalypse.
C. You play as ranch hands trying to get by in the Dust Bowl.
D. You play as a vineyard being invaded by wild dogs.

40

True or false?: The 3rd edition of *FATE* was a departure from being a generic system, and the main book was set in the world of the popular series *The Dresden Files*.

41

When the game publishing company Paizo decided to put out a science fiction game using the Pathfinder rules, what did they decide to call it?

41. *Starfinder.*

39. A. You play as enforcers in a fictional version of the West. 40. False. *The Dresden Files* used 3rd edition rules, but the base game was *Spirit of the Century,* a pulp setting.

9

PIXELATED ROLE-PLAYING

Questions about the Video Games That Were Shaped By—and Helped to Shape—the RPG Industry

It took surprisingly little time for RPGs to invade video games. The first *D&D* video game came to market in 1981, only a little less than a year after *Pac-Man* was first unveiled in Tokyo! While that game, *Dungeons & Dragons Computer Fantasy Game*, was a simple handheld device with a tiny LCD screen in which a tiny sword-wielding hero could painstakingly explore a tiny and fairly simple map full of monsters, the industry has come a long way. Now games show off an extremely detailed tiny sword-wielding hero traversing an extremely detailed tiny map full of monsters and, most recently, become intimately entangled with their party's druid who is sometimes an actual bear.

During the development of these games, there's been 3D maze exploration, first-person shooters, city and dungeon simulators, and even flight simulator games all taking place in the various worlds of *Dungeons & Dragons* and beyond. You'll find all manner of questions relating to video games of today and yesteryear within the pages of this chapter. Today, some of the biggest video games of any given year can come straight from the pages of your favorite tabletop game. The movement has also spread well beyond D&D, with popular and awesome games coming from sources as diverse as Shadowrun, Cyberpunk, Pathfinder, and even a few more niche games such as *Heavy Gear*, *Space 1889*, and *Traveller*.

Total Possible Points: 58

1

There's been a grand tradition of tabletop RPGs becoming video games, and popular video games also becoming RPGs! In 2000, Blizzard Entertainment partnered with Wizards of the Coast to produce *Dungeons & Dragons: Diablo II Edition*, allowing D&D players to take on the roles of Paladins, Amazons, and Barbarians to face down the forces of the Prime Evils of Sanctuary. Which of the following was a downloadable supplement for this exciting game?

A. The Secret Cow Level
B. Tooth & Claw: The Assassin and Druid Guide
C. Heavenly Perils
D. Artifacts of Harrogath

2

Rifts: Promise of Power's video game included a class that was designed to be included in the core RPG. What was the name of this spellcasting class focused on contrasting forces?

1. A. The Secret Cow Level. 2. The Elemental Fusionist.

3

True or false?: *Dungeons & Dragons Online*, a massively multiplayer online game (MMO) based on the 3rd edition *Dungeons & Dragons* rule set released in 2006, features recorded narration in some dungeons recorded by Gary Gygax.

4

Blizzard would continue to work within the framework of Dungeons & Dragons with their other flagship properties, including games set in both the Warcraft and Starcraft Universe. When *Warcraft: The Roleplaying Game* was replaced by the *World of Warcraft: The Roleplaying Game* (yes, there's a difference!), several new classes were added. These classes were an unusual hybrid of WoW classes and classic D&D classes. Which of the following was not a class from *World of Warcraft: The Roleplaying Game*?

A. Paladin

B. Warlock

C. Tinker

D. Necromancer

5

True or false?: The first video game developed by SSI offshoot company Mind Control Software was *Alien Logic: A Skyrealms of Jorune Adventure*, based entirely on an obscure 1980s sci-fi RPG title.

3. True. 4. C. Tinker. 5. True.

SSI, or Strategic Simulations Inc., was a well-known publisher of computer RPGs in the early 1990s. While a great deal of their famous classic titles were based on *D&D*, a few were derived from other, lesser-known TSR products at the time, including the *Buck Rogers XXVC* RPG and campaign setting. One such game received not only a PC version but a slightly stripped-down release on the Sega Genesis as well, in 1991. What was it called?

   A. *Buck Rogers: Matrix Cubed*
   B. *Buck Rogers: Countdown to Doomsday*
   C. *Buck Rogers' Putting Challenge*
   D. *Buck Rogers: The Midnight Time*

Critical Info

The first appearance of Buck Rogers was in a 1929 comic strip, penned by Philip Francis Nowlan, and it eventually spawned more comics, books, television series, movies, and radio serials through the late sixties, though occasional revivals of the comic strip would happen from time to time. When John F. Dille (who syndicated the strip) died, the rights to the character passed over to Lorraine Dille Williams, president of TSR in the 1980s. When she tried to publicize it again, the Buck Rogers of TSR RPGs became a different incarnation of the character based on writings by her brother, Flint Dille, instead of the original Nowlan creation.

7

Canceled in 1997, the game *Werewolf: The Apocalypse* was slated to be the first video game to use a White Wolf RPG license. It was meant to be an isometric 3D beat-'em-up game and the first of a series of collaborations between White Wolf Publishing and Capcom. What systems was it meant to release on?

- **A.** Nintendo 64 and PC
- **B.** Sega 32X
- **C.** Sony PlayStation and Sega Saturn
- **D.** Super Nintendo and Game Boy

8

In the mid-nineties, game developer Capcom would release a pair of hack-and-slash adventure games based on the D&D license still remembered today for excellent gameplay and charming, well-designed characters and enemy sprites. The first was called *Dungeons & Dragons: Tower of Doom*, but what was the name of the second, based on a class D&D campaign setting?

9

What preexisting NPC from the game *Cyberpunk* does Keanu Reeves play in the hit CD Projekt Red Game *Cyberpunk: 2077*?

7. C. Sony PlayStation and Sega Saturn. 8. Dungeons & Dragons: Shadow over Mystara. 9. Johnny Silverhand.

True or false?: *StarCraft*, the Blizzard real-time strategy (RTS) science-fiction series of PC games, had a short-lived game published in and using the rule set of D20 Modern.

While the big names of RPG history have dozens of video games under their belts, there are a surprising number of single video games based on mostly forgotten RPG systems as well. One such game was based on early D&D competitor *Tunnels & Trolls*, and it was generally considered to be the second modern RPG published. What was the name of the 1990 *Tunnels & Trolls* CRPG, published by New World Computing?

A. *Tunnels & Trolls & Tetris*

B. *Sorcerer Solitaire*

C. *Sea of Mystery*

D. *Crusaders of Khazan*

12

True or false?: The MMO *Champions Online*, originally arriving in 2007, is based on the superheroes and powers found in Palladium Games RPG Heroes Unlimited.

10. False. While there was a short-lived *Starcraft* RPG, it was published in and used the rule set of the Alternity engine, rather than D20 Modern. 11. D. *Crusaders of Khazan*. 12. False. It is in fact based on the *Champions* RPG, which is a Hero System product.

13

The tiny creature Boo is a boon companion for Baldur's Gate series' ranger Minsc. This critter, an expert in going for the eyes, is what species?

Critical Info

Minsc and his friend Jaheira are unique in *Baldur's Gate 3* as they are returning playable characters from previous entries. They have, in fact, both been in all three of the Baldur's Gate games. But beyond that, Minsc and his delightful hamster friend are so well liked that they've turned up in more places besides, featuring as NPCs in some campaign guidebooks in RPGs. They have also appeared as Magic: The Gathering cards, allowing you to have "Minsc and Boo, Timeless Heroes" as the leaders of your very own Commander deck!

14

True or false?: Due to some licensing issues at the time, there were only a handful of video games based on the 4th edition *D&D* rule set, including a long-defunct, free-to-play *Facebook* browser game and *Neverwinter*, a very-loosely-based-on 4e MMO that is still available today.

13. Miniature Giant Space Hamster. 14. True.

15

Though the roster is somewhat smaller than in its two predecessor games, *Baldur's Gate 3* has an exceptionally deep level of programming. The game allows you to personalize and give stories to the recruitable party members, with most characters being viable options for romance and all having complex trees of morality (allowing for all manner of interactions). How many recruitable companions are there in the game in total (not counting summonable allies like Us, Scratch, or Fork/Shovel/Basket)?

A. 5   **B.** 6   **C.** 8   **D.** 11

16

There were only two officially licensed video games based on the *Traveller* RPG license, and true to the nature of that unusual game, they featured character creation in which your character could retire and even die in the process. Each was made by Paragon Software for the Amiga, Atari ST, and MS-DOS, and featured real-time planetary and space exploration in addition to ground combat. What was the first game called?

A. *MegaTraveller 1: The Zhodani Conspiracy*
B. *Traveller: Adventures in K'kree Space*
C. *Advent of the Vargr*
D. *Space Winnebagoes*

Connect each of the recruitable NPCs from the classic hit CRPG *Baldur's Gate 2: Shadows of Amn* to their class or classes.

A. Aerie

B. Anomen Delryn

C. Cernd

D. Haer'Dalis

E. Jan Jansen

F. Keldorn Firecam

G. Mazzy Fentan

H. Valygar Corthala

1. Fighter

2. Paladin

3. Cleric/Mage

4. Fighter/Cleric

5. Bard

6. Stalker Ranger

7. Thief/Illusionist

8. Druid

17. A. Aerie & 3. Cleric/Mage. B. Anomen Delryn & 4. Fighter/Cleric. C. Cernd & 8. Druid. D. Haer'Dalis & 5. Bard. E. Jan Jansen & 7. Thief/Illusionist. F. Keldorn Firecam & 2. Paladin. G. Mazzy Fentan & 1. Fighter. H. Valygar Corthala & 6. Stalker Ranger.

18

Though often remembered for its highs in the nineties, the first video game based on a White Wolf *World of Darkness* property wouldn't hit store shelves until June of 2000. Chronicling the journey of the vampire Christof from twelfth-century Vienna to modernish London, what was the name of this RPG?

19

Rifts: Promise of Power was a tactical grid combat RPG set in the Palladium Games Rifts universe, in which you could take control of a Mercenary, Psionic, or Magic-User, eventually unlocking well-known OCC (Occupational Character Class) subclasses from the core RPG itself. What failed system did it appear exclusively on?

20

One of the earliest licensed D&D video games was released on the Intellivision in 1982 under the simple name *Advanced Dungeons & Dragons*, but was later expanded to which name to differentiate it from a newly arrived sequel?

21

True or false?: Drizzt Do'Urden, the famed Drow star of his own series of D&D novels written by R.A. Salvatore, was playable for the first time in the 2000 game *Baldur's Gate 2: Shadows of Amn*.

Critical Info

Drizzt Do'Urden has been around awhile, having been introduced in The Icewind Dale novels in 1988 and starring in the R.A. Salvatore novel *Homeland* (from the Dark Elf trilogy) in 1990. He's appeared in thirty-nine novels, a series of short stories, and the Forgotten Realms Campaign–setting books for *D&D* in the 2nd, 3rd, 4th, and 5th editions. He's a Drow Ranger, but he isn't always *entirely* that. As the editions change, so, too, do his class levels. In the 2nd edition, Drizzt was a level 16 Ranger. In the 3rd, with its access to expanded multiclassing, he was a Fighter 10/Barbarian 1/Ranger 5; in the 4th edition, he was only officially a level 21 Skirmisher foe; and in the 5th edition, he is a level 11 Fighter/level 8 Ranger. Close readings of the books suggest even more class levels.

22

True or false?: Aerie, the Elven spellcaster from *Baldur's Gate 2*, was actually an Avariel, a race of winged Elf that lived in the Forgotten Realms setting. She was just missing her wings.

21. False. While Drizzt made an appearance in the game, he was not playable, and he was a controllable party member in the prior title *Menzoberranzan* on PC in 1994. 22. True.

189

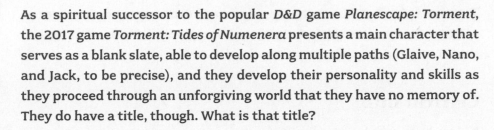

23

As a spiritual successor to the popular *D&D* game *Planescape: Torment*, the 2017 game *Torment: Tides of Numenera* presents a main character that serves as a blank slate, able to develop along multiple paths (Glaive, Nano, and Jack, to be precise), and they develop their personality and skills as they proceed through an unforgiving world that they have no memory of. They do have a title, though. What is that title?

A. The Rising Tide

B. The Last Castoff

C. The Sorrow

D. The Main Man

24

Released to critical acclaim in 2013, *Shadowrun Returns* marked a new look and feel for video games based on the venerable Cyberpunk RPG. With a main character able to choose from five races and a wide array of classless options (from chromed-up street samurais to the spirit-summoning shamans), the RPG was popular enough to spawn two well-received expansions, *Shadowrun: Dragonfall* and *Shadowrun: Hong Kong*. But what was the name of the first campaign that *Shadowrun Returns* shipped with?

A. Dead Man's Switch

B. Blood Relations

C. Regards from the Ripper

D. Project Aegis

23. B. The Last Castoff. 24. A. Dead Man's Switch.

Baldur's Gate 3 is full of all manner of conversant NPCs, and thanks to several of your party members being able to carry on full conversations with animals, the list of creatures you can carry on conversations with is expanded to even greater lengths! What manner of cat is the prim and proper devourer of pigeons (and friend to party Wizard Gale), Tara?

A. Tressym

B. Persian

C. Sphinx (Hairless) Cat

D. Miniature Giant Space Cat

Critical Info

His Majesty, one of the many interactable cats of *Baldur's Gate 3*, is a fan favorite, being so mean and catlike that even if you do cast the Speak with Animals spell before talking to him, you're likely to just get an irritable hiss in response. He is a hairless cat in the game (one of several), though this is an unintentional glitch. He was originally meant to be furry, and at one point plans were announced to patch his intended fuzzy form in, resulting in Internet outcry from fans. The game developer backed off changing the cat, choosing instead to modify the eye color of a different in-game hairless cat so that the two would not be identical.

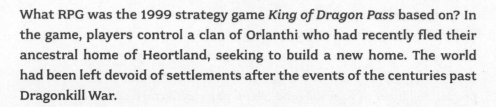

What RPG was the 1999 strategy game *King of Dragon Pass* based on? In the game, players control a clan of Orlanthi who had recently fled their ancestral home of Heortland, seeking to build a new home. The world had been left devoid of settlements after the events of the centuries past Dragonkill War.

A. *Empire of the Petal Throne*

B. *Glorantha*

C. *Mage Knight*

D. *Talislanta*

27

True or false?: *World of Warcraft: The Roleplaying Game*, published by Sword and Sorcery Studios in 2005, had exactly the same playable races as *World of Warcraft* the MMO did at that time.

28

True or false?: The last of the well-known "Gold Box" D&D games for PC was the 1992 title *Treasures of the Savage Frontier,* in which the party is initially summoned to clear the last Zhentarim warriors from the Dwarven city of Llorkh.

26. B. *Glorantha.* 27. False. The tabletop RPG added the High Elf, a species from the previous *Warcraft* games that was absent from the starting roster of "vanilla" *World of Warcraft,* though two variations of the species have become playable since then. 28. False. In fact, the final Gold Box title was 1993's *Forgotten Realms: Unlimited Adventures,* published by Microgames Inc.

29

In Paizo's CRPG *Pathfinder: Wrath of the Righteous*, players not only chose species, class, prestige classes, and other options pulled from the tabletop game but also a new power source known as Mythic Paths. This is a set of new abilities and stories pulled from one of many powerful forces in the world and the worlds beyond. Which mythic path specifically caused all recruitable party members to abandon the player if they were so villainous as to choose it?

A. Azata

B. Lich

C. Aeon

D. Swarm-That-Walks

30

In the PC classic *Planescape: Torment*, based on the *D&D* Planescape campaign setting, your nameless main character can recruit a diverse and unusual cast of characters to join him on his quest to remember who he is and what has happened to him. One in particular is a Modron (a lawful neutral robotic creature from the plane of Mechanus) named Nordom. What specific variety of Modron is he?

A. Quadrone

B. Duodrone

C. Vibraphone

D. Monodrone

A bit of an oddity in the world of D&D video games, the 1992 Nintendo Entertainment System game *DragonStrike* is a top-down shooter in which you, as the pilot, fly your choice of metallic dragon through a series of levels and blast away at evil chromatic dragons. What classic D&D campaign setting does it take place in?

Critical Info

The NES version of *DragonStrike* is an odd duck—it's a port of an MS-DOS game also called *DragonStrike* with a similar story and concept, but different execution. The computer game was a first-person flight simulator, something that the NES was not especially good at. So the NES version was converted to its top-down form remembered today. Additionally, in 1993, the board game/RPG hybrid Dragon Strike was released, intended to be an easy access point for new players to learn about role-playing with a simplified rule system and a number of pre-written quests. It is infamous today for coming with an instructional VHS tape, which features actors playing D&D characters as they battle foes in a story that's not similar to the game it came with.

32

True or false?: The *Fallout: The Roleplaying Game* published by Modiphius Entertainment will let you build and play as a Mr. Handy Robot just like in the famous game series.

33

Connect each video game to the campaign world/planet it takes place on! Be wary, if the title contained the name of the campaign setting, we've stripped that title down to a subtitle to keep things interesting.

A. *Dungeons & Dragons: Warriors of the Eternal Sun* [Sega Genesis]

B. *Dungeons & Dragons Tactics* [PSP]

C. *Dungeons & Dragons Online: StormReach* [PC]

D. *Shadow Sorcerer* [DOS]

E. *Pathfinder: Kingmaker* [PC]

F. *Stone Prophet* [DOS]

G. *Wake of the Ravager* [DOS]

H. *Torment: Tides of Numenera* [PC]

1. Ravenloft
2. 9th World
3. Dragonlance
4. Dark Sun
5. Eberron
6. Greyhawk
7. Mystara
8. Golarion

33. A. Dungeons & Dragons: Warriors of the Eternal Sun (Sega Genesis) & 7. Mystara. B. Dungeons & Dragons Tactics (PSP) & 6. Greyhawk. C. Dungeons & Dragons Online: StormReach (PC) & 5. Eberron. D. Shadow Sorcerer (DOS) & 3. Dragonlance. E. Pathfinder: Kingmaker (PC) & 8. Golarion. F. Stone Prophet (DOS) & 1. Ravenloft. G. Wake of the Ravager (DOS) & 4. Dark Sun. H. Torment: Tides of Numenera (PC) & 2. 9th World.

34

BioWare's 2002 title *Neverwinter Nights* is one of the most well-remembered and award-winning titles in the history of D&D video games on the PC. An isometric 3D perspective, incredible customization options, and a robust set of tools for DMs to use in a complex and comprehensive multiplayer mode were just a few of the charms of the engine. What was the name of the final expansion pack for the game, released in 2004?

35

Praised at the time for its innovative isometric view and wide array of destructive weaponry and possible upgrades, the Super Nintendo and Sega Genesis game *MechWarrior 3050* (1994) was based on the long history of Battletech board games and RPGs, but one divisive element in gameplay was not as well received by reviewers at the time. What was it?

A. The two-player mode involved one player aiming the guns and the other steering the mech.

B. Your playable character options included both humans and the humanoid bird species the Tetatae.

C. The game required a camera attachment to scan box codes of existing models the player owned for upgrades.

D. One secret level was just the mech in a Pac-Man maze blasting ghosts, pretzels, and cherries.

34. Kingmaker. 35. A. The two-player mode involved one player aiming the guns and the other steering the mech.

36

While *Vampire: The Masquerade* wouldn't become a video game until the 2000s, White Wolf Publishing branched out and produced an RPG based on a popular video game much earlier in 1994. This game allowed you to play as your favorite warriors of the world or build new characters that emulated their fighting styles, such as Shotokan Karate, Sambo, and Kabaddi. What was the name of this game?

Which of the following popular video game franchises does not have at least one RPG or RPG campaign setting/supplement licensed from it and based on it?

A. Diablo

B. Everquest

C. Dragon Warrior

D. Street Fighter

True or false?: Had it not been summarily canceled, the first video game based on a White Wolf property would have been *Werewolf: The Apocalypse*, an isometric top-down beat-'em-up to have been published for the Sega Saturn by Capcom until its 1997 cancelation.

36. *Street Fighter: The Storytelling Game.* 37. C. Dragon Warrior. 38. True.

There are an incredible amount of Dungeons & Dragons video games, and not all of them are just digital adventurers going on a D&D-style adventure! Draw a line connecting each of the following officially licensed Dungeons & Dragons video games to its genre of video game.

A. *Shadow over Mystara*

B. *Dungeon Hack*

C. *DragonStrike*

D. *Stronghold*

E. *Iron & Blood: Warriors of Ravenloft*

F. *Neverwinter*

G. *Dungeons & Dragons: Tiny Adventures*

H. *Tales from Candlekeep: Tomb of Annihilation*

1. Roguelike RPG

2. Fighting game

3. Board game

4. Hack and slash

5. Idle game

6. Flight simulator

7. City builder real-time strategy

8. Massive multiplayer online

39. A. *Shadow over Mystara* & 4. Hack and slash. B. *Dungeon Hack* & 1. Roguelike RPG. C. *DragonStrike* & 6. Flight simulator. D. *Stronghold* & 7. City builder real-time strategy. E. *Iron & Blood: Warriors of Ravenloft* & 2. Fighting game. F. *Neverwinter* & 8. Massive multiplayer online. G. *Dungeons & Dragons: Tiny Adventures* & 5. Idle game. H. *Tales from Candlekeep: Tomb of Annihilation* & 3. Board game.

40

The video game *Ian Livingstone's Deathtrap Dungeon*, an action-adventure platformer similar to *Tomb Raider*, was released in 1998 for both Sony PlayStation and PC. It featured two playable characters (the barbarian warrior Chaindog and the Amazon Red Lotus) and was not well received, with reviewers disliking its astonishing difficulty and terrible, obtuse controls. It was based on a single-player RPG, specifically the sixth book in what series of choose-your-own-adventure—styled game books written by Steve Jackson and Ian Livingstone?

A. GURPS

B. Grim Tales

C. Adventuring Heroes

D. Fighting Fantasy

41

What was the name of the main character in the 1994 Sega Genesis *Shadowrun*? He was able to take on the role of Street Samurai, Decker, or Gator Shaman, and adventured in the magically altered Seattle of the 2050s.

10

LAUGHABLE GAMES

Games That Make Us Laugh or Cry (Provided You Sometimes Cry from Laughing)

For as long as people have been writing their own RPGs, they've been injecting a bit of humor alongside. Pop culture references, pun names, and straight-up jokes have permeated the pages of games since the beginning, especially given the rebellious spirit and lack of corporate editing that marked early entries to the RPG genre. *AD&D* is still remembered today for including literal one-panel joke strips alongside the other art.

By the early eighties, comedy games were starting to emerge as a genre all their own, and as of today, several of them have become so popular that the genre is viewed as on par for quality and respectability as horror, superheroes, cyberpunk, or even fantasy. Of course, all of those genres appear in the comedy scene too, and these games will be featured with questions of their own in this chapter. Each genre has its own send-up books, which are just about the most common form of comedy game, whether it be the sci-fi computer dystopia taken to its illogical extreme of *Paranoia*, the horror-but-make-it-silly excesses of games like *Don't Look Back* or the *RPG-13 B Movie Horror System*, or the wacky cartoon worlds of *Toon*, comedy as a genre is established, and there is no shortage of hilarious options. Throughout this chapter, we'll take a look at some of the games that have made us laugh over the decades, or at least made us cringe.

Total Possible Points: 58

1

The history of humor-themed RPGs starts out pretty rough, with the first game designed exclusively to be a funny role-playing game quickly being banned from GenCon (the largest American RPG convention) in 1982. It was banned for explicit content detailing sex, drugs, crime, death, and pregnancy in the average Canadian high school. It also featured art by early D&D illustrator Erol Otus. What was it called?

A. *Alma Mater*

B. *Over the Edge*

C. *Mustang Summer School*

D. *Graduation*

2

Though this game started out as a relatively serious story about survival and power in the post-apocalypse, over each subsequent edition it would gain more elements of humor and satire. It would eventually continue into its current 7th edition, in which it isn't weird to launch a raid on the rabbit guards of a long-abandoned moon base, while you play as a single character that is composed of a swarm of tiny yeti.

A. *After the Bomb*

B. *Apocalypse World*

C. *Gamma World*

D. *The Xro Dinn Chronicles*

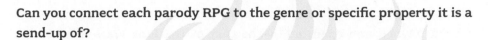

3

Can you connect each parody RPG to the genre or specific property it is a send-up of?

A. *ACE Agents*

B. *Staged Heroism*

C. *Extreme Vengeance*

D. *Konosuba: God's Blessing on This Wonderful World*

E. *X Crawl*

F. *It Came From the Late, Late, Late Show*

G. *Flabbergasted!*

H. *Paranoia*

1. Isekai and light novels

2. Bad horror movies

3. Violent TV game shows

4. The Venture Bros

5. The Roaring Twenties

6. Sci-fi dystopias

7. Eighties action movies

8. GI Joe

3. A. *ACE Agents* & 8. GI Joe. B. *Staged Heroism* & 4. The Venture Bros. C. *Extreme Vengeance* & 7. Eighties action movies. D. *Konosuba: God's Blessing on This Wonderful World* & 1. Isekai and light novels. E. *X Crawl* & 3. Violent TV game shows. F. *It Came From the Late, Late, Late Show* & 2. Bad horror movies. G. *Flabbergasted!* & 5. The Roaring Twenties. H. *Paranoia* & 6. Sci-fi dystopias.

4

Name the Skipray Blastboat ship (a piece of Expanded Universe Star Wars fiction) owned and operated by the cast of the Star Wars–themed AP podcast *Campaign*.

5

True or false?: In the school comedy RPG *Hellcats and Hockeysticks*, set in a fictional British boarding school, the only two kinds of playable exchange students are samurai and ninja.

6

What was the name of the home campaign setting created by influential comic author Jolly Blackburn, creator of *Knights of the Dinner Table,* for his D&D campaign? Hint: He would go on to name his publishing company AEG after it.

In 1987, TSR would publish *The Book of Wondrous Inventions*, a supplement to *D&D* that added a variety of inventive new magical items to the game. Most of these items would be found somewhat frivolous by the average 5th-level barbarian, consisting largely of goofy gnome versions of modern home appliances and other electronic conveniences. Which of the following was NOT a published magic item from this wacky tome of wonders?

A. Melrond's Foolproof Dishwasher
B. Fiendish Exercise Machine of Bardolpho the Mad
C. Damos' Ball of Bowling
D. Grandalf the Green's Portable Putting Hole

Critical Info

The Book of Wondrous Inventions was so delightfully silly that it's worth the time to just list a few more of the wacky gadgets to be found in it. There's Blashphor's Ever-Vigilant Baby Cradle and Nursery, a self-rocking massive cradle designed to contain twelve infants and entertain them with a motion-activated lullaby-singing parakeet; Honest Obie's All-Night Armor Merchant, an enormous box that calculates the value of proffered scrap metal from an adventurer and pays out gold for it, before magically smelting it into new armor; and even Brandon's Bard-in-a-Box, which is...a magical boombox. When the game was written in the eighties, "guy with boombox on shoulder in public" was still the height of hilarity in sight gags.

8

True or false?: The sci-fi RPG *Human Occupied Landfill* is printed in the highly comedic font Comic Sans.

9

Heralded as the first generic cartoon RPG, *Toon* is a game about shenanigans, both caused and endured. With a focus on emulating classic *Looney Toons*—style shorts, the game allowed you to play as nearly anything that could turn up in a cartoon, pull ladders out of your back pocket, openly flout the laws of physics, and never really die. What company was the publisher of *Toon*?

A. FASA

B. Amarillo Design Bureau

C. Steve Jackson Games

D. Palladium Games

10

True or false?: The first real human to appear as art on a Magic: The Gathering card was the music artist Post Malone.

8. False. *Human Occupied Landfill* isn't actually printed in any font, unless "scans of actual bad handwriting" counts as a font, in which case it's printed in that one. Yes, the game is entirely handwritten, which makes the experience of reading it interesting, to say the least. 9. C. Steve Jackson Games. 10. False. The first real human depicted on a Magic: The Gathering card is Albert Einstein, on the card Presence of the Master from the 1994 Legends set. This means the card is about one year older than Post Malone himself.

11

A classic anecdote was told by game designer and voice actor Richard Aronson and first appeared in the pages of the Amateur Press Association (APA) *Alarums and Excursions* somewhere between 1985 and 1986. This anecdote featured a character encountering what he perceived to be a deadly foe, calling out to it, firing arrows at it, and eventually, fleeing from it for his life. The joke has since appeared in *Call of Duty Black Ops II*, *Final Fantasy XIV*, and *RuneScape*. What was the "deadly foe"?

12

In 1986, Lee Garvin wrote a fantastical comedy RPG featuring transdimensional portals dumping all manner of drunks, private eyes, toughs, wizards, and general ne'er-do-wells into a space adventure of cosmic proportions with a twist. This game always started with everyone meeting up at the game's eponymous bar. So what was the bar called? Complete the name: *Tales from...*

A. *Genesis Space*
B. *The Dude and Catastrophe*
C. *The Hyperspace Lounge*
D. *The Floating Vagabond*

11. A Gazebo. 12. D. *The Floating Vagabond.*

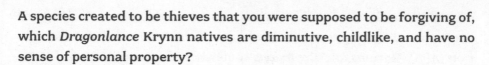

13

A species created to be thieves that you were supposed to be forgiving of, which *Dragonlance* Krynn natives are diminutive, childlike, and have no sense of personal property?

14

True or false?: The *D20 Modern* RPG supplement *Urban Arcana* snuck in pictures of cult classic cartoon character Zorak from *Space Ghost* (and his hit talk show *Space Ghost Coast to Coast*) in art of one of the monsters, the Living Dumpster.

Critical Info

The *Urban Arcana* supplement had a fairly sharp sense of humor. The conceit for the game's main campaign setting was that most humans simply lacked the magical sense necessary to notice that the world around them was full of monsters. People would automatically explain away anything supernatural they saw with a false mundanity instead. Dragon fire? No no, exploding gas station pump. One of the funniest elements was the local McDonald's equivalent, which was run entirely by demi-humans and monsters as a job creation network for creatures living in a world that would hate them if they could see them. The toys in the kids meals were actually magic (if you were able to see or access magic in any way)!

15

First published in 1995, this comedy game in which you play as cavemen who are stuck with incredibly small vocabularies (seventeen words at first, though eventually expanded to eighteen over future editions) was hilariously lethal, with characters easily dying to other cavemen, falling rocks, dinosaurs, and simply being too dumb to try things (like swimming out of a river). It was named after a simple caveman-style utterance, but which one?

A. *Land of Og*
B. *Land of Ugg*
C. *Kingdom of Zug Zug*
D. *How is Babby Formed*

16

What is the highest secret information clearance level available to Troubleshooters in Alpha Complex, the central city of the sci-fi dystopian RPG *Paranoia*?

17

True or false?: The apocalyptic RPG *TORG*, about multiple invading universes converging on Earth, has an acronymic title, which stands only for *The Other Roleplaying Game*.

18

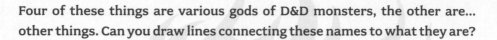

Four of these things are various gods of D&D monsters, the other are... other things. Can you draw lines connecting these names to what they are?

A. Sseth

B. Psilofyr

C. iKlax

D. Koka-Nola

E. Ilsensine

F. Sekolah

G. Phosex

H. Shungite

1. Monster God (Myconid)

2. Long-lost Coca-Cola competitor

3. Carbon-rich black stone considered a healing crystal in the New Age community

4. Pharmaceutical calcium acetate supplement

5. Monster God (Sahuagin)

6. Monster God (Mind Flayers)

7. Monster God (Yuan-Ti)

8. Computer sound file format

18. A. Sseth & 7. Monster God (Yuan-Ti). B. Psilofyr & 1. Monster God (Myconid). C. iKlax & 8. Computer sound file format. D. Koka-Nola & 2. Long-lost Coca-Cola competitor. E. Ilsensine & 6. Monster God (Mind Flayers). F. Sekolah & 5. Monster God (Sahuagin). G. Phosex & 4. Pharmaceutical calcium acetate supplement. H. Shungite & 3. Carbon-rich black stone considered a healing crystal in the New Age community.

19

The 1990s saw the rise of the dark disaster comedy in theaters. In this genre, selfish yet inept characters would be rapidly undone by a spiral of events from their greed, including such well-remembered films as *Fargo*, *A Simple Plan*, *Suicide Kings*, and *Very Bad Things*. This genre would go on to inspire an RPG about events spiraling out of control in deadly and humorous ways, which would be published by Bully Pulpit Games in 2009. Can you name the game?

A. *Go*

B. *Ever Widening Gyre*

C. *Fiasco*

D. *Hard Luck Heroes*

20

Games that are parodies of other, more popular games are practically a staple of the RPG humor field. There are a number of games that take to task the foibles, unclear rules, silly stories, and self-seriousness of industry juggernauts. Which of the following parodies isn't a real example of a game designed to take potshots at a larger RPG (or more than one!)?

A. *Dungeons: The Dragoning*

B. *Katanas & Trenchcoats*

C. *TWERPS*

D. *Sense & Sensibility & Superspies*

19. C. *Fiasco*. 20. D. *Sense & Sensibility & Superspies*.

21

Of the various comically powerful shticks in the 1991 comedy RPG *Tales from the Floating Vagabond,* which one would allow you to shoot anyone, regardless of their cover or your ability to see them, but not actually kill anyone...unless it was high noon?

22

Written by the same man (Mike Pondsmith of *Cyberpunk* fame) who wrote the very first anime RPGs, this game is well known now for being much older than the current American understanding of anime tropes. The game features magical girls that are actually wizards and a greaser-themed rockabilly high school setting that is super fun and zany, but not necessarily connected to today's anime. Written in 1987, can you name the first humor game inspired by anime tropes?

A. *Mekton Zeta*
B. *Teenagers from Outer Space*
C. *Ranma One Third*
D. *Hot Gundam Summer*

23

True or false?: The Flumph, a sort of morally upright flying psychic jellyfish monster from Dungeons & Dragons, unofficially both moves and attacks by farting.

24

Though he was a mighty and capable ranger, the character Minsc and his boon companion Boo from the Baldur's Gate video game series were always a little silly. He was definitely a source of comic relief in the long and complex game series and often spouted bold and alarmingly goofy catchphrases at any moment. Which of the following is not a Minsc original catchphrase?

A. "Fool me once, shame on you. Fool me twice, WATCH IT! I'm huge!"
B. "Sleep with one eye open, evil! Maybe both."
C. "Less prattle, more battle!"
D. "Float like a flumph, sting like an ixitxachitl!"

Critical Info

Our editors told us to avoid spoilers, but there's some funny comedy stuff throughout *Baldur's Gate 3* that we just had to share with you. So first of all [redacted], until midway through Act 3 at which point [redacted]'s butt, causing [redacted] to emit [redacted], which of course is illegal, but [redacted] to the left, so [redacted] and [redacted], using all three of the frogs. So good, right?

23. True. 24. D. "Float like a flumph, sting like an ixitxachitl!"

25

Who is the king that all kobolds must hail no matter what other mischief, crime, or laziness they are currently up to in the fantasy comedy RPG *Kobolds Ate My Baby*?

26

True or false?: In the 3rd edition printing of the *Tomb of Annihilation* adventure for Dungeons & Dragons, the hidden door to the dungeon was made of solid steel and included a note stating that it wasn't made of a more valuable metal anymore because the creators were tired of adventurers stealing it.

27

True or false?: Game of Thrones author George R.R. Martin's book series *Wild Cards* was actually based on his personal *Heroes Unlimited* RPG campaign.

25. King Torg. 26. True. 27. False. Wild Cards began as a campaign Martin played in Chaosium's *Superworld* RPG engine, not the Palladium *Heroes Unlimited Game*.

214

28

The Adventure Zone, a popular podcast in which the three McElroy brothers (and their dad) play RPGs and get into hilarious predicaments, has branched out into a sprawling media empire including all manner of merch and comic book stories. But it is itself a spinoff, based originally on a single filler episode of their other longer-running podcast. What is that show called?

A. *My Brother, My Brother, and Me*
B. *Sawbones*
C. *The McElroy Zone*
D. *System Mastery*

29

In which Pinnacle-published RPG were the long-dead Hoomanrace lost in the big flush, paving the way for all manner of surviving things to become the dominant intelligent creatures of the world, including sentient boogers, snack cakes, cockroaches, and more?

30

An improvisational comedy podcast set in a fictional fantasy world (though not using any particular RPG engine), *Hello from the Magic Tavern* rarely gets going to anywhere, choosing instead to linger in the tavern itself with such fun characters as Arnie and Chunt. They are also joined by Matt Young's character Usidore the Blue, a wizard of some repute and magnificence. Which of the following is NOT one of Usidore's titles or secondary appellations?

A. Manipulator of Magical Delights
B. Zoenen Hoogstandjes
C. Prestidigitator Par Excellence
D. Champion of the Great Halls of Terr'akkas

31

A pastiche of *Highlander* and *Vampire: The Masquerade* with a thick layer of sarcastic edge plastered over the top, the game *Katanas & Trenchcoats* is full of deadly immortals that are powered by their perfect katanas, wicked catchphrases, and impressive outfits. What city does the game largely take place in?

Can you name a duo composed of a famous NPC wizard from a *D&D* campaign setting and that NPC's creator, who would often write stories in which his wizard character would come to visit him in the real world for drinks and conversation?

A. Raistlin Majere & Margaret Weiss

B. Elminster & Ed Greenwood

C. Ssaz Tam & Jeffrey Donovan

D. Jon Irenicus & Anomen Delryn

Critical Info

He may not meet his own creations for drinks, but RPG designer and all around cool guy Keith Baker, creator of the Eberron campaign setting for Dungeons & Dragons, is also deeply involved in his own creation. He has moved away from Wizards of the Coast and into his own company and designs, but he still releases occasional updates on lore from his world, answers questions to fill in holes in the map from interested fans, and even takes to social media in cosplay as characters from the world. He shows the coolest looks (and surprisingly well-photoshopped magical effects) of the steam and magic punk-esque world of Eberron.

True or false?: There is an RPG based on the furry world webcomic *Kevin & Kell*, in which you play as the denizens of Haven, the strip's world of carnivores and herbivores living together and going to work, school, and so on as humans do. Despite the relatively real-life banal nature of the webcomic, the game is heavily combat focused.

34

What comedy troupe released a sketch that made popular meme slogans out of such phrases as "I'm attacking the darkness!" and "Roll the dice to see if I'm getting drunk"?

A. The Whitest Kids U Know

B. Critical Role

C. Dead Alewives

D. The Frantics

35

True or false?: The character played by Marlon Wayans in the movie *Dungeons & Dragons* (2000) was a thief named Smiles.

33. True. 34. C. Dead Alewives. 35. False. His character was a thief, but his name was Snails, thank you very much.

218

36

Who is the host of the eighteenth season of Dropout's Dimension 20 show, known as *Dungeons & Drag Queens*?

37

Dragon is a long-running magazine full of adventures, game options, interviews, and all manner of other topics of interest to gamer nerds. It served as a home for a number of the biggest and most influential of the RPG print comics of the day during its long run from 1976 to 2007 (and is now online-only). One notable comic was the venerable *Dork Tower* by John Kovalic, though it didn't actually get its start in *Dragon*. Where did it start?

A. *Shadis*

B. *Owl and Weasel*

C. *Polymancer*

D. *Tower of Dorks*

38

Examining the bounds of what an RPG can be, this game by James Wallis for Hogshead Press largely consists of telling stories to the other players until one of them dares call you a liar.

36. Brennan Lee Mulligan. 37. A. Shadis. 38. The Extraordinary Adventures of Baron Munchausen.

219

Which one of the following D&D monsters was really included in the 5th edition adventures *Descent into Avernus*, and featured leathery semi-functional wings, an insatiable lust for meat, and a life cycle that began with budding and eventually dropping off of a disgusting infernal tree onto the hard ground below?

A. Abyssal Chicken
B. Batclops
C. Hooked Chain Duck
D. The Unicornugon

True or false?: Palladium RPG *Teenage Mutant Ninja Turtles and Other Strangeness* was originally printed with a deeply offensive section that classified homosexuality as a psychosis that player characters could contract due to random rolls.

41

Connect each cleric to their respective podcast, show, or campaign setting.

A. Durkon Allotrope

B. Piffany

C. Dee

D. Bellow

E. Yvonnel Baenre

F. Dorian

G. Jozan

H. Lando

1. *Rude Tales of Magic*

2. *Nodwick*

3. *AD&D 3rd Edition Player's Handbook*

4. *Knights of Badassdom*

5. *D&D: Wrath of the Dragon God*

6. *Rat Queens*

7. *Order of the Stick*

8. *Forgotten Realms*

41. A. Durkon Allotrope & 7. *Order of the Stick.* B. Piffany & 2. *Nodwick.* C. Dee & 6. *Rat Queens.* D. Bellow & 1. *Rude Tales of Magic.* E. Yvonnel Baenre & 8. *Forgotten Realms.* F. Dorian & 5. *D&D: Wrath of the Dragon God.* G. Jozan & 3. *AD&D 3rd Edition Player's Handbook.* H. Lando & 4. *Knights of Badassdom.*

ABOUT
THE
AUTHORS

Jon Taylor is a professional podcaster from San Diego. He has a degree in English literature from the University of California, Santa Cruz. He spent several years as a stand-up comic on the East Coast before moving back to Southern California. Jon is the coauthor of *Düngeonmeister: A Drink Master's Guide*. Jon is also a cocreator and cohost of the *System Mastery* podcast with Jef Aldrich, in which they review and comment on odd classic RPGs, poking fun at obscure stories and systems while taking the games for a spin.

Jef Aldrich is a professional podcaster from San Diego. Along with Jon Taylor, he has been building a podcast brand outside of the big network channels. Jef started entertaining people as a SeaWorld tour guide and eventually just started being funny for a living on his own. Jef is the coauthor of *Düngeonmeister: A Drink Master's Guide*. He is also a cocreator and cohost of the *System Mastery* podcast with Jon, in which they review and comment on odd classic RPGs, poking fun at obscure stories and systems while taking the games for a spin.

Level up your campaigns with our Düngeonmeister series!

Pick up or download your copies today!